The Possible Dream

ten who dared

The Possible Dream

ten who dared
by Marthe Gross

CHILTON BOOK COMPANY

Philadelphia   New York   London

For my Family

"Be all you *can* be. . . ."

—From a National Library Week Theme

Life is not easy for any of us. But what of that?
We must have perseverance and above all confidence in ourselves.
We must believe that we are gifted for something,
and that this thing, at whatever cost, must be attained.

—Marie Curie

Foreword

In the pages that follow, you will meet ten Americans who are "superstars" in their chosen fields. These ten decided "to go for the big one"—and made it.

How did they reach the top rank in their fields? Was it hard or easy? What criticism and discouragements did they face and overcome?

As you read their stories you will see that the success these ten now enjoy came to them only after the most rugged trials and failures.

The teen-age figure-skating champion who won the only gold medal awarded to an American at the 1968 Winter Olympics was the same girl who placed sixth in 1964—and took a fall on the ice in full view of royalty.

The young biologist who became co-discoverer of the structure of DNA (nucleic acid) and winner of a Nobel Prize was cut off from his fellowship because his research goal was considered a "dead end."

A dancer now acclaimed for his work in television and on Broadway as well as in ballet had to stop lessons at a critical age and leave the field in order to study marine transportation.

These ten Americans come from widely varied backgrounds: the Far West, the slums of Cleveland, the South, small-town New England, a middle-class neighborhood in the Bronx. Whatever their background, though, you will see as you read their stories that they all have certain things in common:

They discovered when they were young that doing a particular thing—their "own thing"—in sports, science, music, or another field made them feel intensely alive and deeply satisfied. They derived a special excitement from this that came in no other way.

They were determined to excel: They studied, probed, practiced until they had mastered their field completely.

They knew they would make mistakes—and were patient with themselves when they did.

They had unshakable faith in their own future—even when no one else believed in them, when others discouraged them or scoffed at their ability.

These ten know the excitement, the thrill, of achievement. But they know, too, the struggle—physical and mental—that the young person faces when he decides to "go for the big one."

In trying and failing as well as in trying and succeeding these ten show us what it takes to reach . . . The Possible Dream.

Garden City, N.Y.   *Marthe Gross*

Acknowledgments

I am sincerely grateful for the cooperation of the following individuals and organizations: Bob Banner Associates; Mr. and Mrs. Bill Moyers; Wells, Rich, Greene, Inc.; Mr. Neil Simon; S. Hurok Associates; Mr. Edward Villella; Mrs. Doris Fleming; Mme. Natalie Molostwoff; the United States Lawn Tennis Association; Dr. Harold S. Turkel; Mrs. Margaret Driggs; Mrs. Joan Lindroth Angerer; McCann-Erickson, Inc.; the Interpublic Group of Companies, Inc.; and the research staffs of Hofstra University and of the Garden City and Hempstead, N.Y., libraries.

Marthe Gross

Contents

The Possible Dream

ten who dared

"Icy Elegance" on the Tennis Court

Arthur Ashe, Jr.

Sweat trickled into the corner of his eye. He blotted it with his wristband and, crouching, sidled into place behind the base line. Across the net, his opponent tossed the ball into the air, rocked back and served. The ball skimmed the net and blurred past. He lunged at it—but too late. He couldn't get a racket on it.

"Point, game, match to Mr. Laver," called the referee.

With the racket bumping at his side, he walked to the net to shake hands with Rod Laver. First round—and he was eliminated!

People back in Richmond would read about it in the paper the next morning and say, "Thought that sixteen-year-old Ashe boy could play better tennis than that! Went up there to Forest Hills in New York and thought he was gonna take 'em—and they bumped him out in the first round. First round!"

Arthur Ashe, Jr. walked slowly, numbly toward the locker room. Around him on all sides were the immaculate grass courts of The West Side Tennis Club. Tanned boys in white shorts and shirts, girls in white tennis dresses were playing out matches against their first-round opponents.

Threading his way past court after court, he heard the *pock!* of the ball against racket gut and the applause of the spectators. It was late summer, 1959—tennis season at Forest Hills, New York.

How beautiful it was! How elegant: the West Side Tennis Club in late summer. Red roses, velvety lawns, clipped hedges. Negro waiters in starched white jackets serving cool drinks. The ivy-covered Tudor clubhouse with its high-peaked tile roof commanding an expanse of courts. And at the opposite end, the stadium where the giants of world tennis had played: Bill Tilden, Bill Johnston, Don Budge, Jack Kramer, and Pancho Gonzales.

Arthur Ashe, Jr., sixteen years old, from Richmond, Virginia, threading his way past the tennis courts, saw it all in a blur as he headed for the showers. Tomorrow he would be home with his daddy on Sledd Street in the five-room frame house with the oak trees in front. He could unwind there, be himself. This world of tennis, dominated by whites, would be 300 miles away. More like three million. Three billion.

Would he ever make it in tennis? Would he ever come here and play a decent match? Or was he kidding himself? Other Negro players from Virginia had shown plenty of determination when they were in their teens, but had lost hope and finally dropped out. They were driving cabs now in Lynchburg and Richmond. Or mopping floors.

Who was to say that he'd be any different? . . .

Tennis had started for him ten years ago at home in Richmond. His father, Arthur, Sr., was a special police officer in charge of discipline at Negro playgrounds in the city. In one of them—Brook Field—there was a house which went with the job. The Ashes and their two sons, Arthur, Jr., and John, the baby, lived in this house.

Surrounding it on all sides were ball fields, basketball courts, an Olympic-size swimming pool—and tennis courts. There were four old tennis courts perhaps a minute's walk from the side door of the Ashes' house.

For six-year-old Arthur, life in Brook Field was heaven. He was a shy child, so thin that his legs and arms looked like rubber hose. But he was sharp about rules, and his reflexes were good. Even the big fellows said the kid picked up a game fast. With the sights and sounds of sports floating into the house morning, noon, and night, he absorbed sport techniques almost through his pores: shooting baskets, lashing a baseball, whipping a racket at a tennis ball.

The ball made a certain sound when it was hit right: *pock!* The men who came to play on the courts outside his house would smash the ball back and forth across the net. *Pock!* Sometimes they played far back against the screen, sometimes they went up close to the net to smash the ball hard before it could bounce. *Pock!* Arthur loved that sound.

One day he borrowed a racket and a ball—gray and with not much bounce left in it—and began hacking around the hard-surface courts. He was six years old and the racket was too big and heavy, but he kept at it.

His father bought him a cheap racket of his own after a month or so, and he dragged it around the courts looking for a partner. Once in awhile an older boy would hit some easy balls to him. Arthur would lift the racket and swing— *whoosh*—batting empty air. Once in perhaps a dozen tries the racket would connect. Then he got the thrill that kept him trying for another hour—and another.

The summer he turned eight he began watching closely when big fellows played. One of them, an eighteen-year-old named Ronald Charity, was really good. He was a student at Virginia Union College and a part-time playground instructor. He moved lithely and stroked the ball with a smooth, fluid motion. To eight-year-old Arthur he looked like a champion.

Ronald Charity had never had any tennis lessons—he had taught himself the basics from books like Lloyd Budge's *Tennis Made Easy* and Bill Tilden's *How to Play Better Tennis.* "It just happened that I could pull off a page and project into my imagination how it should be done," he once explained.

Since his college was only a few blocks from Brook Field, Ronald practiced there early in the morning before classes and again in the evening. He noticed that whenever he came he had an audience of one: the skinny little kid who lived in the playground house. When the kid came onto the courts it was hard to tell whether "he was lugging the racket or the racket was lugging him," he said later.

It was obvious that the child loved tennis. He had a narrow, delicate face with eyes that took in every move with foxlike quickness.

One day he blurted his question: "Would you show me how to play?"

Ronald Charity put the racket in his hand and showed him how to grip it. Then, standing six feet away on the same side of the net, he began to throw balls to him.

"That's it, keep your eye on the ball," he called gently. "Keep your body sideways to the net. Sideways, Arthur.

"Once again, now. Let's see you bend those knees. They're full of jelly, they're mush. That's right, swing now— arm straight—and follow through."

The next evening Ronald found his "student" waiting for him.

"I practiced on the backboard today," Arthur told him.

"Good boy! All right, let's see if you remember what I taught you yesterday. Show me how you hold the racket."

It became a ritual. Every evening that summer Ronald Charity worked out with Arthur, throwing balls and teaching the basics of a stroke, then going to the other side of the net to develop it in actual play.

"When the stroke had been taught, I would cross the net and hit it with him. We practiced cross-court forehands, forehands down the line, cross-court backhands. We played every summer evening. The little guy caught on so quickly," Charity recalled later.

As the young college man watched Arthur play tennis he began to see unusual qualities in the boy. He was quiet by nature and much better disciplined than other eight-year-olds. His mother had died when he was six. Her loss, coupled with his father's deep concern for his two sons, had made him a serious-minded youngster.

There were hours of sport and play for both of the Ashe boys all summer. But they knew, in the marrow of their bones, that they must never wander from the Brook Field playground without getting permission from the house-keeper, Mrs. Berry, or from their father if he happened to be at home.

Years later, when Arthur Ashe, Jr. was named to the Davis Cup team, he was asked about his strict upbringing. He answered that his father was "firm but fair."

"I never once in all my life talked back to my father," he said. "My younger brother, Johnny—he's in the Marines now—he'd question him sometimes and I'd shudder. I'd feel awful if I ever did anything at all bad that my father found out about. He trusts me completely."

The day that young Arthur was to enter the Baker Street Grammar School his father walked with him to the building. "Walk along now at your own speed," he told his son. As he studied the boy's gait, he fell into step beside him. When they arrived he looked at his watch. "Ten minutes to get here," he announced. "When school lets out I want you home in ten minutes—not eleven. No excuses!"

There were times in the years to come that Arthur was tempted to dawdle on the way home or go off to a friend's house six blocks away. But his father's orders were indelibly marked in his mind. Mr. Ashe was not harsh with his sons. He loved them deeply and had great hopes for them. He would pour thousands of dollars from his modest salary into expensive sports equipment for them in the years to come. But discipline came first. In his work as a police officer, he had seen too many boys—some of them as smart as Arthur and John—sent to reform school for shoplifting, vandalism, or "borrowing" a car on impulse.

This would not happen to his sons. He was a jovial man who smiled a lot and joked easily. But deeply rooted in him was a fierce determination: His sons would not ruin their lives by making impulsive mistakes.

When Arthur was eleven some of his friends had newspaper routes. He wanted one too, but he was turned down. Mr. Ashe thought it was too dangerous.

"I kept the children pretty close to home," he said later. "My children never roamed the streets. A regular schedule was very important. A parent has got to hurt his own child, discipline him, hold him back from things you know aren't good for him."

So there was strict discipline in Arthur's life, but it was tempered by his father's deep love and a childhood that was ideal except that it lacked a mother.

Looking back on it when he was a lieutenant at West Point, he said, "I didn't live in a so-called ghetto situation. I never saw rat-infested houses, never hung out on corners, never saw anyone knifed. We were never poor, not even close. Things weren't that tough for me. I've never had a job in my life. In a way, I envy people who have had. The field behind my house was like a huge backyard. I thought it was mine. Brook Field was just an athletic paradise, a dream world for a kid who liked to play sports. Tennis, baseball, horseshoes, basketball, football, swimming—you name it. The pool was so full of kids in the summer you couldn't see the water. I had no problems at all. There was really no reason in the world for me to leave the place. Everybody came to me. The athletic equipment was kept in a box in my house."

One day Ronald Charity told Arthur that he was organizing a little tennis tournament for the kids who had been playing at Brook Field. "You should enter, Arthur. You'd have a good chance."

He entered at age eight but lost to an eleven-year-old. But losing didn't bother him at all. He entered tournaments at other Negro parks in Richmond and began winning.

For his ninth birthday an aunt and uncle pooled their money and gave him his first really good racket, one that cost $22.50. His game was improving nicely and Ronald Charity made a big decision. . . .

In Lynchburg, Virginia, lived a man with a dream—Dr. R. Walter Johnson. Doctor Johnson, a Negro general practitioner, loved tennis so ardently that he had become a missionary for it. His home, a rambling brown-and-white frame house, was converted every summer into a tennis camp for Negro boys and girls who showed promise. If he accepted them, they would come for two months of tennis lessons and free room and board. In return, they were to do chores: water the lawn, weed the garden, and—the job that daily fell to Arthur and one he came to loathe—hose out the doghouse.

Every summer Doctor Johnson accepted six to eight promising youngsters, hoping that his regimen of tennis lessons, concentrated practice, and strict training would put them in a class where they might compete against white youths of comparable age.

Running such a free camp was costing Johnson a lot of money—but he did it willingly. He hoped that a few of the boys or girls would somehow reach the heights attained by a girl he had coached in the late 1940s: Althea Gibson. Althea had come from New York's Harlem to get lessons at Doctor Johnson's tennis camp and gone on to be national women's champion. Success like that made it all worthwhile.

Ronald Charity called Doctor Johnson and told him about Arthur. The older man knew Ronald—and every other promising Negro tennis player in the South—and trusted his judgment. He agreed to give the boy a trial. When school was out for the summer, Arthur packed his bag and went with his father to the bus station, heading for Lynchburg.

As the bus pulled out, the boy turned and waved. His father waved back.

"Good-bye, Daddy."

"Good-bye, Arthur."

There would be a thousand partings between these two in the years to come. The frail ten-year-old riding away on the Lynchburg bus would someday travel by jet to Spain, Sweden, Australia. He would be driven to Wimbledon in a limousine from his London hotel to play tennis before royalty. But that morning the longest journey in the world was the three-hour bus ride into the Virginia Piedmont, through Prince Edward County, then past Appomattox to Lynchburg.

He was met by an assistant to Doctor Johnson and taken to the doctor's big house on Pierce Street. It was a homey place swarming with activity. Arthur and three other boys —all older and better players—were lodged in the upstairs bedrooms. (Two girl trainees lived with friends of Doctor Johnson's down the block.)

All six were kept on a strict tennis regimen from morning until night. They got up at eight, fixed breakfast for themselves, and straightened their rooms. Then, changing to the all-white clothes that are traditional for tennis, they went out on the court to practice.

The right clothes were important, Johnson felt, even when his young trainees were practicing early in the morning in the sweltering Virginia summer. He was a stickler for thoroughness: You approached tennis—if you wanted to go for the Big Goal—the way a medical student approached a lesson in anatomy. It was very serious business. You did not cut any corners.

Mornings out on the court were routine: The trainees spent three hours, from 8:45 until almost twelve, hitting to each other without keeping score. After lunch and a rest each drilled on his weakest stroke: One might do 100 serves, another 100 backhands or cross-courts.

Chores also had to be worked into the afternoon schedule. "Somebody had to cut the grass, tend the roses. Somebody had to clean out the doghouse—with lye," Arthur recalled later.

Although he disliked the chores at the doctor's big house, there were plenty of compensations. The meals were sumptuous: platters piled high with meat and unlimited servings of rice—Arthur's weakness. "I was a little saddened that we were never allowed ice cream, soda pop, or pastries. But I stuffed myself with meat and rice every night," he said.

Doctor Johnson watched his trainees' table manners carefully. They were not allowed to snatch bread or elbow a tablemate out of a last pork chop. Manners were part of the long-range strategy Johnson had worked out: When his trainees were playing whites in the top tournaments they would have to remember that they were being watched and judged. He didn't want white tennis officials sneering at his protégés because their manners weren't polished. Manners were as important, he said, as wearing tennis "whites."

He also instilled in the trainees the habit of underaggressiveness. "If a ball lands an inch outside the line, play it— don't argue," he told them. When he spoke, the trainees listened. His words carried authority.

He was also an excellent tennis teacher. Usually by 4:30 in the afternoon he was finished with patients and paid a visit to the court to see at firsthand how the trainees were doing.

"You're breaking your wrist on the forehand," he would call.

"You're not tossing the ball high enough when you serve."

"On the backhand you're swinging late."

When supper was over he would go down in his basement den with the trainees and show tennis films or talk strategy. This was also the time when Arthur and the others studied the tennis rulebooks. Homework on the rules was a must. Doctor Johnson gave exams on them.

Spindle-legged Arthur Ashe did not impress Walter Johnson as top tennis material that first summer. But he had a willingness to pitch into practice that was appealing. He hustled.

"Arthur was quick, he had fast eyes—and he worked harder," Doctor Johnson said about the frail beginner.

When summer ended, Arthur went home to Richmond with an invitation to come back to tennis camp the next year. (Maybe a new trainee would be around then to clean out the doghouse!)

Summers at Doctor Johnson's were to become a fixture in the life of Arthur for the next seven years. The coaching he received there could not have been surpassed anywhere in the South—and it was free. Tennis expenses can be astronomical: lessons run as high as $10 or $15 an hour. Rackets and restringing may cost $500 a year. Shorts, shirts, tennis shoes and socks wear out at an alarming rate. When a boy starts playing in tournaments someone must put up the entry fees and supply him with traveling expenses.

Arthur's father was determined to carry as much of this burden as he could. He took on extra jobs—washed windows, cut grass, scrubbed floors—so that his son could have $40 rackets for this sport he loved.

But there was a limit to what he could spend. He had remarried after five years as a widower, and his second wife and her son and daughter by a previous marriage had to be provided for. He also had to plan for young John's future. The money—wherever he could earn it—had to be spread in many directions. Not all of it could go to Arthur.

Walter Johnson knew that Arthur's father was in a financial bind. He believed in the boy's potential enough, though, to dig into his own pocket. "Doctor Johnson must have plunked down more than $3000 from his own pocket giving me the kind of help that young white players in Richmond get automatically from the tennis patrons," Arthur said in a later account of those days.

The Lynchburg doctor believed that money invested in young Negro athletes would bring more satisfying returns than in banks or the stock market. It could change their lives. They might not play at Forest Hills or Wimbledon like Althea Gibson. But for some there was always the prospect of getting tennis scholarships to college. More than 100 of his protégés had done just this. Watching Arthur develop, summer by summer, he was sure the boy could win a college scholarship too.

If Arthur could just prove himself on the tournament circuit. . . .

Arthur had his first taste of tournament competition during his second summer in Lynchburg. Doctor Johnson wanted him to "get his feet wet" by playing in the tournaments sponsored by the American Tennis Association, a Negro counterpart of the U. S. Lawn Tennis Association. Playing in the under-twelve division, he licked every opponent he faced!

The next year he won the ATA National Championship for boys under thirteen and began taking competition in stride. Doctor Johnson would pack up Arthur and his other trainees in his big car and head for a tournament. One weekend it would be Baltimore, the next Philadelphia or Washington. He had close friends in all those cities and they welcomed his tennis kids warmly and gave them a bed and hearty meals.

Doctor Johnson had his eye on the big tournaments sponsored by the USLTA. He dreamed of seeing his young Negro hopefuls play the best in the country. But before he brought them in to play white boys with white umpires before white crowds he wanted to be sure that they had plenty of tennis ability—and "cool."

"Stifle your reactions," he told his trainees. "Never complain when you're out there on the court. And call close ones *against* yourself. If a ball lands even an inch outside the line and there's no linesman assigned to your match, play that ball."

Tennis is known for its spoiled "brats." Temper tantrums erupt at every big match. Sixteen-year-olds stamp their feet, hurl rackets, even shake the backstop in rage when points go against them.

Doctor Johnson had seen too much of this behavior by hotheaded white boys. He was determined that his young

Negro trainees would be different. "When you play in a match, be polite," he told them. "You'll make mistakes. Everybody does when they're under pressure. But don't blow up. Don't rant and rage. Keep your temper under control. Smile."

It was hard advice to take. Arthur wanted to win those points as much as any opponent. But he saw the long-range wisdom of keeping his emotions under control. He schooled himself to be icy-cool on the court. Winning or losing, he made his face a mask. Steel nerves came to be his trademark. In years to come a magazine would state, "Arthur Ashe, Jr. plays with icy elegance."

His emotional control was so complete that it came to bother some opponents. "I think he works too hard trying to keep his cool," Clark Graebner, a tennis rival, told a reporter. "He comes off the court after winning a title and gives it the cool play. It's not human to be that cool!"

But the "cool play" was just what the doctor ordered.

The summer Arthur was fifteen, Doctor Johnson made several efforts to get him into USLTA tournaments and succeeded. In one—the New Jersey Boys' Tournament—he reached the semifinals. In Maryland, going against a field of 150, he won the state title. Most importantly, he was allowed to play in the junior national championships at Kalamazoo—the Forest Hills of the youth circuit—and reached the semifinals.

Kalamazoo is a showcase. Many college coaches go there yearly to study the new crop of tennis players. One coach, J. D. Morgan of UCLA, watched fifteen-year-old Arthur Ashe play and made a mental note: good potential; if he continued to develop he might be worth a tennis scholarship.

The next year, when Arthur, now sixteen, came back to Kalamazoo, his game was off—he reached only the third round. But J. D. Morgan was again watching. He studied Arthur's serve (strong). His volleys (weak). And his

backhand—that backhand was wicked! When it was working right, the kid could lash the ball almost the way Pancho Gonzales did.

He sought out Doctor Johnson and began asking questions: Who was Arthur, exactly? What about his parents?
How did he do in school?

Walter Johnson answered the questions straight. No em-
bellishments. All the years he had been coaching Arthur he
had hoped and prayed something like this might happen—
that one of the country's top tennis coaches might consider
the boy for a college scholarship. But he was not one to
count chickens . . .

Late that summer came Arthur's first big test at Forest
Hills, New York. There at the exclusive West Side Tennis
Club, the USLTA holds the *big* championships. Players who
have been toiling on the tournament trail for months come
to Forest Hills in late August and early September to slay or
be slain.

To sixteen-year-old Arthur Ashe, the grass courts fanning
out from the beautiful high-peaked clubhouse glittered with
glamor. This was the big league of tennis—the place where
Tilden had played. Budge. Kramer. And Pancho Gonzales
—Arthur's hero. Pancho had come to Forest Hills in 1948—a
twenty-year-old from the Mexican section of Los Angeles—
and romped through the competition.

Maybe, Arthur thought, he could pull some surprises too.

But it was not to be. A boy from tropical Australia, Rod-
ney Laver, breezed through him in the first round.

"Point, game, match to Mr. Laver."

Numbly he shook hands and headed for the showers.
Around him on all sides, sixteen- and seventeen-year-olds
were playing out their matches on the grass courts. *Pock!* A
forehand smash. *Pock!* Service ace.

"Beautiful shot!" called the spectators. "Way to go!"

This was Forest Hills, the world series of tennis. How
many of the hopefuls playing around him would be good

enough to compete in the stadium court at the other end? Dennis Ralston. Chuck McKinley.

Arthur Ashe? Maybe. Maybe not!

When Arthur had completed his third year of high school at Walker High in Richmond, Doctor Johnson got a call from a tennis booster in St. Louis. Richard Hudlin, a Negro teacher who had once captained the tennis team at the University of Chicago, was inviting Arthur to live at his home in St. Louis that winter so that he could play on the indoor courts there. If Arthur really had style he could certainly sharpen it by playing such stars as Cliff Buchholz, Chuck McKinley, Dick Horwitz, and Jim Parker.

It was a rare opportunity. A solid year of intensive coaching and practice against the hottest young tennis stars in the country was too good to turn down. Doctor Johnson said yes.

Arthur swallowed hard when he heard the decision.

Summer in Lynchburg and on the tennis circuit; winter and spring at home in Richmond—this had been the pattern for seven years. The rhythm of it felt right to Arthur. He liked going to Walker High and playing trumpet with a few buddies in a little "combo."

He was starting to date a bit and get around to parties. Not too many, though. His father believed that a seventeen-year-old should be home by eleven most nights.

The only time Arthur missed the deadline was when a school official's daughter invited him to a party at her home. When he failed to come home at eleven, Mr. Ashe drove to the girl's home, rang the bell and asked for his son. The girl stared at him with contempt, then turned and called in a loud voice, "Here's your ancient father, Arthur!"

Discipline and deadlines. His daddy believed in them. It did not matter what other people said. Arthur Ashe set the rules for the family and through the years they had worked out fine, whether the boys were at home or away. He had been sure of this when he put his ten-year-old on the

Lynchburg bus. And he was sure of it now that Arthur was going to live in St. Louis.

Life with the Hudlins meant training much stricter than Arthur had known even in Lynchburg. Doctor Johnson was a tennis patron. Richard Hudlin was almost a zealot. He saw in Arthur a Negro athlete who could be the Jackie Robinson of tennis: a superstar who would someday challenge the best white players. He planned, consequently, a routine that was make-or-break.

Arthur described it later in dry terms. "I did push-ups every morning, went to school until noon, then played tennis all afternoon. And after tennis I ran a mile."

There were other problems. A tennis-playing friend who was white invited Arthur to play at a private tennis club one afternoon. Arthur was on the court ready to serve when a voice called out, "Hey, you! Get off there. We don't allow colored in this club."

Without a word Arthur left.

From the time he was a small boy, he had heard his father say, "Respect everybody, whether or not they respect you. And don't hold a grudge. I've seen too many Negroes wreck their lives through hating whites."

Respect everybody . . . whether or not they respect you.

Sometimes it was hard.

In the west end of St. Louis, on a rise overlooking Forest Park, stands Washington University. There, on the campus courts, Arthur played on sunny afternoons with the full encouragement of Washington University's athletic officials. When the weather turned cold, Richard Hudlin took him downtown to Market Street where the 138th Infantry Armory had five indoor courts. Before the year was out he had mastered playing tennis on wood.

"I got some wallop into my forehand and I began to rush the net more often," Arthur recalled later. "Wood is a fast surface, so I had to build the big-serve-and-volley game. Playing for years on a clay surface had made me a retriever, a pusher. But you don't win by pushing the ball on hard-wood or cement."

Larry Miller, the armory pro, was his coach. Miller's coaching led the way to Arthur's first big title. In November, when the national indoor championships were held at the St. Louis Armory, he took the Junior Indoor Championship from top-seeded Frank Froehling, two years older than he. The score was 6-4, 16-14, 9-11, 3-6, 6-1 in a rugged battle that lasted more than four hours!

The following May he went to Charlottesville for the National Interscholastic championships and beat Cliff Buchholz and Jim Parker in the last two rounds to take the title.

"I guess Doctor Johnson and Mr. Hudlin were mighty pleased. It proved that what they had done for me wasn't wasted," he commented in his story, *Advantage Ashe*.

In June he graduated from Sumner High School in St. Louis at the top of his class. Scholarship offers had been coming in from several top schools: Harvard, Michigan, Arizona, and Michigan State. But the one that was irresistible was postmarked Los Angeles—an offer from J. D. Morgan to attend the University of California at Los Angeles on a tennis scholarship. Arthur was elated. "It not only had a high academic rating but a high tennis rating," is the way he put it. "Year after year its tennis teams were at—or near—the top in college competition. Offering me a chance to play there was like offering a football player a chance to play at Notre Dame."

With his father's blessing, he enrolled at the giant West Coast university and began the last stage of training that would take him to the pinnacle of tennis.

As it turned out, UCLA was the perfect choice for Arthur for several reasons. The California sun warmed and relaxed him after all the years of pound-it-in training. There was an easy, jog-trot rhythm about classes, term papers, library research. Enrolled as a major in business administration, he found that he was well able to keep up with assignments except when the tennis team was away from Los Angeles for extended tours.

But UCLA was geared even for this. Generous alumni had donated money for tutors so that star athletes could make up their missed lectures. Without pouring too much effort into studies, he averaged B−.

The best thing about UCLA, of course, was that he was a full-fledged member of one of the country's top tennis teams. It gave him a sense of belonging that he had never had before. When Arthur arrived on the big campus at age eighteen he had been playing tennis for more than ten years. But he had been a loner, a sharp young Negro athlete from the South, not completely comfortable at the exclusive white tennis clubs.

"It's an abnormal world I live in," is the way he once put it. "I don't belong anywhere. It's like I'm floating down the middle. I'm never quite sure where I am."

Out on the court, with a racket in his hand, Arthur could lose himself in sport. But even there his mind wandered sometimes and he developed the bad habit of letting down at a crucial point in a match.

The really bad times came, though, after a tournament would end. When he had to go back to a strange room in a strange town loneliness seeped in like fog through a cracked windowpane.

All the ringing phrases of encouragement he had heard through the years would come to mind:

You've got the stuff, Arthur. You'll be one of the top-seeded players in this country someday.

You'll be the Jackie Robinson of tennis. Just hang in there.

You're a pioneer, Arthur. You'll show 'em all someday at Forest Hills.

Staring at the ceiling in the dark, remembering the phrases—and trying to believe them—he would click on his radio and find a station at the far end of the dial. He could almost always pull in a Negro station that played records he loved. Rhythm and blues was the best remedy he knew—for the blues.

The years as a lonely teen-age athlete ended when Arthur came to UCLA. He was a member of the Bruins, one of the great college teams, and life opened out with explosive activity. He joined a Negro fraternity and became a brother to some of the star athletes on campus. Invitations poured in for parties—with no eleven-o'clock curfew. In his spare time he roughhoused with his room-mate and costar, Charles Pasarell—"Charlie Possum," as he was called—and played billiards and ping-pong with other friends.

J. D. Morgan, the tennis coach and later athletic director at UCLA, was a dynamo who barked at his players when they slacked off or were lackadaisical as Arthur could be. But he was not a slave driver. "J. D. believed in training, but he never tucked his players in bed at ten o'clock," is the way Arthur put it.

Some of the world's best pro stars lived in the Los Angeles area. Pancho Gonzales was only four blocks away from the campus. Morgan made a point of inviting them to come to the UCLA courts to play regularly with his team members. Arthur Ashe playing with Pancho Gonzales—it was a dream come true!

He began to see his strengths and weaknesses as never before. Topping the list of strengths was his backhand. When he was seven and eight years old Ronald Charity had made him concentrate on it even more than his serve or forehand. Then Doctor Johnson had insisted that he hit hundreds and hundreds of backhands on sticky summer afternoons in Lynchburg.

Working out with a player like Gonzales, Arthur learned just how deadly his backhand could be. Time and again he lashed a ball so hard that it torpedoed past Gonzales and dusted the chalk line!

His serve was formidable too. The motions were deceptively simple. He bounced the ball twice, tossed it about three feet above his head, arched his body and cracked the ball. *Pock!* It smoked over the net.

Pancho Gonzales, who could crack a ball at 112 miles an hour and whose serve was the terror of tennis in the late 1940's and early 1950's, found that Arthur was acing him more and more in their practice games.

"He's got the best serve in tennis since mine," he admitted. "He just has to build up the game to go with it."

That meant practicing on weak strokes: the forehand and especially the forehand volley. Systematically he worked on them under the warm California sun. With J. D. Morgan coaching and teammates like Dave Reed, Dave Sanderlin, and Charlie Pasarell analyzing his weaknesses—and hitting to them in practice games—he sharpened every stroke.

What he mastered on the campus courts he packed into his suitcase when the Bruin team went out to play tournaments.

"At one time or another I won every college tournament that UCLA entered," he later wrote. "As a senior I won both the Intercollegiate Singles and Doubles."

By the summer of 1963, at the end of his sophomore year, Arthur had climbed to the rank of 18th in the national senior men's amateur division.

In mid-June he boarded an overseas plane for the first time and headed for Wimbledon. With other top U. S. players he entered the tournament at the venerable English stadium, where 128 players from all over the world compete annually for world tennis crowns.

In *Advantage Ashe*, Arthur compares "Wimbledon Fortnight" to World Series fever in America: "The matches are televised all over Europe. You go on the streets and people recognize you. Make a phone call and the operator knows your name."

The first morning the Americans were to play, a sleek limousine, chauffeur-driven, called at their hotel and drove them "through meadows and trees to Wimbledon Township, where the All-England Club is. . . . People were crowded there getting autographs. We felt like movie stars."

Wimbledon was older and more glamorous than any tournament in the States.

"All the magnificence and efficiency dazed me a little," he wrote later. "I felt jittery when it was time for my first-round match." He defeated players from Brazil and Australia but was eliminated in the third round by Chuck McKinley, who went on to win the tournament.

An invitation to visit Sweden with two other American players came at the end of the Wimbledon trip. Arthur flew first to Copenhagen for sight-seeing and then to Bastad, a Swedish resort famed for its tennis. The fact that he was a Negro had always made him an outsider in certain parts of the United States. But in Sweden, his face was an asset. The Swedes studied the tall (6′ 1″), lanky, cocoa-skinned athlete with the flattop haircut and easy smile and welcomed him warmly. On his twentieth birthday, the tournament committee surprised him with gifts and hearty congratulations.

When he got home to Richmond he told his father, "I was a unique item. . . . I enjoyed every hour of it."

The travels which had begun so modestly for Arthur at age ten on the bus from Richmond to Lynchburg were now on a global scale.

Appointment to a coveted place on the Davis Cup team came late that summer. Though he was to play only one match—against Venezuela—he won it in straight sets. Several months later when the 1964 rankings were released, Arthur Ashe had jumped from 18th to 6th!

At the Eastern Grass Court matches the following August, he came face to face in the semifinals with a player who had jinxed him for years in intercollegiate competition: Dennis Ralston of the University of Southern California's powerful Trojan tennis team. Arthur defeated him and went on to lick Clark Graebner in four sets in the finals to take the title.

The next year he climbed to number 3 in U. S. tennis, behind Chuck McKinley (of St. Louis) and Ralston. He was now one of the stars of the tournament circuit. Like other tennis "amateurs" in America, he was entitled to generous expense money for playing the big tournaments.

"Tennis," Arthur told a newsman, "has introduced me to a certain standard of living: plenty of travel, good accommodations, expensive entertainment, quality clothes. More than that, it's given me an entrée to all sorts of places and people. It's been a kind of apprenticeship in good living, and I'm not going to let it all go when I quit. My education gives me a license to look around for the future, and I'm looking around all the time. I'll keep living up to this standard after I quit tennis, because I intend to land a good job."

He had been signed by three firms—Wilson Sporting Goods Company, Coca-Cola, and the Fred Perry sportswear company—to represent them informally. He agreed to use the products of each company whenever he was photographed or when he appeared at social functions tied in with tournaments. In return for such nonstrenuous services he regularly received a moderate check ("retainer") from each firm.

Checking his bank balance, Arthur discovered that he could afford a sports car and a motorcycle. The years of practice and strict discipline were paying handsome dividends!

In late August, 1965, he entered the Nationals at Forest Hills for the last time as a college player. In the quarterfinals he defeated the national champion, Roy Emerson of Australia, in four sets and the gallery of 11,000 spectators in the big stadium gave him a standing ovation, roaring their delight for fifteen minutes.

Meeting with reporters later, Arthur said, "You guys are more excited than I am. . . . One match doesn't prove anything. You have to establish a *trend* of winning. That's what Emerson has done."

The next day, in the semifinals, he lost to Manuel Santana. Fans who had seen him play sensational tennis one day and only fair the next argued hotly. Was Ashe going to make it big or fade away? What would happen when he finished out his last semester at UCLA and left J. D. Morgan's coaching? More specifically, what would he do in Australia that winter, playing the powerful Aussie Davis Cup team? He had faced Emerson—"Emmo"—at Forest Hills and blasted him off the court. But could he do it again or had that been a fluke?

The answer came that winter. During a tour of Australia, Arthur beat Emerson in five sets at Brisbane and a few weeks later in Adelaide topped him in four sets to win the South Australian championship. The powerful Aussie star broke his "Ashe jinx," however, on January 31, 1966, when he beat Arthur in the finals of the Australian singles championship at Sydney.

"Ashe muffed it badly," declared a sportswriter. "He was batting simple returns into the net. The American just wasn't concentrating."

Not concentrating. J. D. Morgan had warned him about that time and again at UCLA. "You've got to give one hundred per cent if you want to win!" he had told Arthur countless times.

Some tennis players could do it. Cliff Richey was one. Cliff was Arthur's room-mate on the tour and he was a tiger for bearing down. Clark Graebner was another player who could concentrate savagely on his tennis.

But fans who had followed Arthur's career knew that on days when he let his mind wander during a match he was doomed. If he was ever to play at Forest Hills again—and get to the *final* round—he would have to cultivate what the fans call "killer instinct."

The last nine credits Arthur needed for graduation at UCLA were taken in the spring semester, and in June, 1966, he graduated with a bachelor's degree in business administration. That summer he fulfilled his Reserve Officer Training Corps obligation—six weeks at camp in Oregon—and was commissioned a second lieutenant in the Adjutant General's Corps in February, 1967. His assignment: Systems Analyst stationed at the U.S. Military Academy at West Point.

For the next year most of his tennis was limited to coaching cadets at the Point. Tournament appearances were spotty—and unimpressive.

"Lt. Arthur Ashe had a disappointing season," one sports columnist wrote late that summer. "He's deskbound at West Point and undertennised. Fans don't expect much of him until his Army service is over."

Fortunately the prediction was only partly true. By spring, 1968, he had begun to ease into serious tennis practice again. Fans saw flashes of the sensational backhand and deadly serve. He flew to England in June and reached the semifinals at Wimbledon before losing to Rod Laver. And in August, he won the U. S. Amateur Championship at the Longwood Club, Boston. Sportswriters began to call him "King Arthur."

"If he plays at this pace at Forest Hills, he's sure to reach the finals," a sports magazine predicted.

Forest Hills in 1968 was historic: For the first time the USLTA was changing to an open tournament. The best pros in the world would compete openly with the top amateurs.

It opened with fanfare and spectacle that reminded many fans of the excitement of Wimbledon. Some of the great stars from the 1940's and '50's were competing: Bobby Riggs, Pancho Segura, Frankie Parker, Ken Rosewall—and the big Californian, Pancho Gonzales.

Sportswriters had predicted that professional stars would dominate, but the opposite was true. By the semifinal round, all but two of the pros had been eliminated: Ken Rosewall of Australia and Tom Okker of The Netherlands. The winner of their match (it was to be Okker) would play Arthur Ashe on the center court of the big stadium.

The day of the men's finals every seat in the big stadium was taken. Arthur's father was there and so was Doctor

Johnson. In the press section sat Pasarell, Graebner—a Davis Cup teammate—and Donald Dell, the Davis Cup nonplaying team captain.

Reporters who had written thousands of words about the "icy cool" of Arthur Ashe, Jr., watched him closely for a clue to his feelings. He walked stiffly to the base line. The pressure of this big one was beginning to tell already. Sweat trickled into his eye, and he blotted it with the wristband. Then, bouncing the ball twice, he tossed it into the air and cracked it. *Pock!*

Somewhere in the stadium, Pancho Gonzales studied the serve. "Ace him!" he muttered under his breath. In the next four hours, Arthur would ace him again and again as he battled one of the shrewdest strategists in tennis.

The first set went to 14-12 before Arthur took it. In the second, Okker took the offensive and won, 7-5.

When the spectators applauded a good shot, Arthur could hear the quickly hissed coaching of Graebner and Pasarell:

"Spin it."

"Move your feet, Arthur!"

"Get your first serve in."

"Bend your knees!"

They wanted him to win. How they wanted him to win this first U. S. Open championship!

Arthur took the third set, 6-3, but Okker was a tough competitor. He came back to take the fourth, 6-3, and even the match.

"Get your first serve in!" hissed Clark Graebner, the man who had faced Arthur the day before in the semifinals and been beaten.

Arthur's flat backhand was working perfectly in the fifth set. He slashed the ball across the net and it spit into the dust a fraction beyond Okker's racket. He had the young Dutchman on the defensive now.

He began blasting the ball past Okker for point after point. Okker's forehand drives came smoking over the tape, but Arthur covered the court with rangy strides and cracked the ball back.

With the score 5-3 in Arthur's favor in the fifth set, he played the last game with a power that capsuled everything he had learned through the years. The lessons from Ronald Charity, Walter Johnson, Larry Miller, J. D. Morgan, and Pancho Gonzales were all in it. He was using strokes shaped on a thousand sweltering afternoons in Richmond, Lynchburg, St. Louis, Los Angeles, Sydney, Brisbane—and Forest Hills, years before, when a lonely sixteen-year-old came to play at The West Side Tennis Club for the first time.

"Game, set, match to Mr. Ashe!"

A roar went up from the stadium. Arthur shook hands with Tom Okker at the net as newsmen surged forward to photograph him: the first amateur to win a major open tournament in America, the first Negro to capture the U. S. Men's Singles title.

In the crowd that swirled around him he looked for one face. When his father shouldered his way through they embraced. Then Arthur Ashe, Sr. did something very unusual for him: He started to weep.

The floors he had scrubbed, the windows he had washed, the sacrifices he had made through the years to give Arthur a chance to be a champion had all been worthwhile.

"That Nader Wouldn't Let Up.... He Wore Us Down!"

Ralph Nader

At 8:55 on a wintry Friday night in 1963, the closing chimes began to sound in a Hartford, Connecticut, department store. Sixteen-year-old Cathy T. and her mother, who had been Christmas shopping, walked out the side exit and across the parking lot to the family car.

A light snow was falling from the December sky, and Cathy's mother pulled out slowly to keep from skidding. With other shoppers now inching their cars out all around her, she headed cautiously for the curving access road that would take them to the highway—and home. Suddenly headlights glared through the windshield. Without warning, a car in the opposite lane skidded on the slushy road and crashed head on into theirs. Cathy hurtled forward, hit the instrument panel, and died of a fractured larynx. Her mother, badly cut on the arms by glass, was pulled from the front seat, dazed and bleeding. The man driving the other car was bruised and emotionally shaken but otherwise unhurt.

A police car arrived, then an ambulance. A stretcher was laid out to receive Cathy's body. On other access roads in the big shopping center, families heading home after Christmas shopping slowed their cars to stare. The dome light twirled in slow crimson circles as attendants lifted Cathy's body through the wide back door of the ambulance. A moment later it drove away in the snow.

"Wonder how it happened?" mused a boy in a passing car.

"Crazy driving!" his father declared. "Somebody's been

out drinking, probably. That's the way accidents happen!"

A great many people traveling the road that night likely expressed the same conviction: Someone had been drinking —or driving recklessly. That was the way most accidents happened. Most people in America that winter of 1963 believed it without question.

One of the few who did not was a serious young Connecticut lawyer named Ralph Nader. His convictions about auto safety challenged almost everything the public believed and the automakers professed.

He accepted the fact that a major part of all auto accidents could be traced directly to the driver. Either he was operating the car at excessive speed, or he was not in responsible control of it—he had been drinking, taking drugs, or was emotionally upset.

But what about accidents like the one that took Cathy's life?

Mrs. T. was an excellent driver. The road conditions that night were hazardous, but she was careful to adapt her driving "to the condition of the road." She cut her speed to 15 or 20 miles an hour. The car that hit hers was going perhaps 30 miles an hour. In technical terms, Mrs. T's car decelerated from 20 miles per hour to zero in a fraction of a second. When this happens, the passengers continue moving through space. ("Bodies in motion tend to remain in motion," states a fundamental law of physics.)

If there is something sharp in their path, flesh and bone slam into it with force that can bruise cruelly—or kill.

That Friday night Cathy hurtled against an instrument panel that was knife-sharp. It took her life.

There were accidents like this every season of the year in Connecticut. Ralph Nader had studied dozens of them since setting up his law practice in Hartford, the state capital of Connecticut. Some clients he represented in court had been injured in similar crashes. A few had been hurt in mysterious one-car accidents—while they were driving along a good road in broad daylight a wheel had collapsed! Or a powerful gust of wind had sent the car swerving out of control and slammed it into a stone wall.

Who—or what—was to blame in these cases? Could it be the automobile itself? Was it really as protective of passengers as it could be?

Six years before, when he was in law school, Ralph Nader had been driving from Hartford to Boston. His car was stopped by police barriers put up at the scene of a tragic accident involving two cars. The glove compartment of one had sprung open in the force of the crash, and a little girl had been almost decapitated when she hurtled against its edge. He never forgot that sight. . . .

Professors at Harvard Law School gave Nader's class an assignment shortly afterward: They were to research and prepare a detailed analysis of several auto accident cases. As he worked in the law library, studying case after case, he was amazed to find that American law courts took it for granted that people were entirely to blame when an accident occurred.

Was the car crashworthy? That question was seldom raised. The courts' attitude could be summed up in the old saying, "Cars are safe enough. It's the 'nut' behind the wheel that causes accidents!"

It infuriated Ralph Nader. Was human life of less value than *cars?* Every year car accidents claimed increasing numbers of lives. They were the single biggest killer of people 5–30 years of age—and the fourth heaviest killer of all age groups. Was *all* this bloodshed traceable to the "nut" behind the wheel?

He was sure it was not. People had come to his law office in Hartford and, sitting across the desk from him, had poured out stories of auto accidents that had taken the life of a son or daughter or put a husband in a wheelchair for life:

"We were on our way to Willimantic. Just outside town I put the brakes on, but the pedal went all the way to the floor. We couldn't stop! I guess I blacked out. The next thing I knew, the police were there and somebody was putting my husband in the ambulance. We had brake fluid—the police checked later and found that we did—but something awful strange happened with those brakes."

As the tall, thin lawyer listened intently, he took notes. *The pedal went all the way to the floor.* The phrase rang a bell in his mind. In the stacks of highway accident reports that he scanned every month there were reports of failure just like this. Highway-safety experts in other parts of the country had checked on this mysterious brake failure and theorized that at certain temperatures the fluid would vaporize. A driver would push down on the pedal and find that it flattened to the floorboard without checking the onrushing speed of the car. Yet, later, when the car was examined—at cooler temperature—the fluid would appear in perfect condition.

Safety experts called this kind of mechanical failure a "phantom killer."

Could accidents like *this* be blamed on driver failure? Yes, said the courts. The law assumed that the owner of a vehicle was responsible for any injury it caused to persons or property.

If steering failed and a car jumped a curb killing people at a bus stop, or if transmission or brakes failed and a car plowed through a store window killing shoppers, the law held the owner responsible.

To Ralph Nader the system seemed outrageously one-sided. The more he talked to clients and the more he read about damage suits—usually against the driver even when there was overwhelming evidence of car failure—the madder he got.

On the floor of the U.S. Senate, early in 1957, Lyndon Johnson, then a Senator from Texas, had called for action to stop "the deadly toll of highway accidents whose very familiarity has bred either contempt or indifference."

He concluded, "We cannot abolish the automobile, but neither can we ignore the problems it brings to us. There is a responsibility here which we must face."

The "we" that Lyndon Johnson referred to was the national government, which progresses like a massive piece of machinery that heaves and shudders, moving with maddening slowness. In 1957 it was not programmed to act positively on safety standards for passenger cars.

It was up to the states to do the job. Or it was left to individuals.

Could an individual—one man working alone, without an organization to back him up—cut through contempt and indifference and rouse the public to demand safer cars? The odds against it were staggering. This lawyer with deep-set eyes that bespoke his Arabic heritage was a modern David going against not one Goliath but three: the indifferent public, the uncommitted government, and the tough-minded automakers, the most powerful group of industrialists in the world.

Most people would have considered it an impossible job to tackle alone. But lives were being lost that might be saved through certain structural or mechanical changes in the automobile. That fact gnawed at Ralph Nader. He was not sure he could rouse people to ask for those changes, but he had to try.

In the same way that a lawyer plans a case before going to court, Nader began planning his one-man safety crusade in autumn, 1960. First, he pored over law journals for news of any damage suits that might be pending against carmakers. There weren't many. Occasionally, though, someone was injured so pitifully through no fault of his own that he did bring a lawsuit. In California a woman had had her arm severed when her car spun out of control and flipped over. Her lawsuit had been settled out of court. In Chicago a man was suing for a flip-over accident that had made him a quadriplegic. In South Carolina the parents of a girl who was impaled against a gearshift lever were also suing. Nader watched these cases with intense interest to see if they would set a precedent.

Early in 1962 he began writing magazine articles about safety. Although he was busy with law clients every day and was teaching history part time at the University of Hartford, he also managed to speak on safety to civic groups in Hartford and in nearby Winsted, Connecticut, his hometown.

But he wanted to do more. Maybe the way to make the general public more conscious of safety was to work through the lawmakers. Every time he had the chance he went up to the state capitol in Hartford and testified before legislative committees investigating highway safety.

Hearing that lawmakers in the neighboring state of Massachusetts were also holding hearings on highway safety, he went to Boston late in 1963 at his own expense to testify at the capitol there. But he was received coldly.

"You say you're from Connecticut," barked one man. "Well, what the devil are you doing in Massachusetts?"

What *was* he doing in Massachusetts? He was trying, in a small way, to help people get improved lifesaving features in the cars they bought. He was also trying, in a small way, to make them aware of their rights as consumers.

In a small way. Perhaps that was the key to his failure. Everything he had done in the past five years—writing, speaking, testifying—had been done either at the local level or to a limited audience. A few thousand people at the most knew of his campaign.

He was not slinging deadly stones at his target giants; he was peppering them with gravel!

If his efforts were to count, Ralph Nader realized, he would have to leave Hartford and go to Washington to lobby as forcefully for his cause as the big industrialists did for theirs. How would he start? He was not sure. Opening a law office in the nation's capital would be costly. Besides, he did not want to practice law at this point; he wanted to change the law, reform and humanize the whole legal concept of car-owner liability.

Taking the safety campaign to Washington meant risking everything he had built since law school. If he failed he would have to start over again from scratch. Was it worthwhile? Or was it a wild-goose chase?

Pulling up roots to search for a better way is a tradition with the Nader family. Forty years before, Ralph's father had left his home in Lebanon on the extreme eastern shore of the Mediterranean to come to the United States. The goal of Nathra Nader and his wife, Rose, was to build a good life for themselves and the children they hoped would be born to them in America.

They picked the pretty town of Winsted, Connecticut (population 10,000), for their home and opened a restaurant. Customers soon discovered that almost every meal at the "Highland Arms" came seasoned with peppery opinions on politics. Nathra Nader had strong feelings about how his adopted country was being run. If a customer happened to look up from the front page of his newspaper between bites, he could expect pointed comment from the man behind the counter!

A newspaper reporter who has lived in Winsted many years once remarked, "There's a saying in town: 'If you go into Nader's restaurant you get ten cents' worth of coffee and a dollar's worth of conversation!' "

In characteristic Arabic fashion, Nathra Nader had intense feelings about political and patriotic matters. People had to care! It was not enough to live passively in the United States, taking democracy for granted. People had to work for justice if democracy was to be saved. He believed it with all his heart and preached it fervently—in Arabic and English—to his children.

Ralph, the youngest child, was born February 27, 1934. Like his older brother and his two sisters, he was a good student. On graduation from the Gilbert School in Winsted, he attended Princeton University on a scholarship.

In 1951, when Ralph arrived at the 205-year-old campus in New Jersey, he found his fellow students happily conforming to tradition. It was Ivy League all the way. The tweed-jacketed young men who were his classmates were thoroughly satisfied with Princeton and the economic system they would soon be part of. They had not the slightest inclination to protest anything. If, on rare occasions, they did have doubts about the ultimate values and goals of American society, they kept quiet. Very aptly these college men of the 1950s were called "The Silent Generation."

To Ralph Nader, whose lively Lebanese-American family had never been cool or silent about anything, the high-conformity Princetonians looked a bit laughable. There was the business about white buck shoes. Everyone on campus wore white buck shoes in the 1950s. Ralph wore blacks, browns, tans—anything that came to hand in the jumble on the closet floor. Shoes, after all, were merely foot coverings to take him across campus from dormitory to classroom. He could not get excited about them.

He did get excited, though, about other matters at Princeton. The groundskeepers were spraying trees and shrubbery with a powerful chemical that had just come on the market: DDT. It did its primary job of killing insects but was so potent that it also killed scores of birds.

Ralph protested hotly in letters to the university paper, but the editors shrugged him off. Their attitude was, Why get bothered about a few dead birds?

Something that worried him even more was the way students could be expelled by officials without a chance to appeal the decision. Ralph felt they should have the right to a review, at least. What he had in mind in 1954 was not a "confrontation" similar to the stormy campus riots that erupted a dozen years later. He believed in orderly change. Authorities at Princeton would consider liberalizing the rules if enough students cared and approached them in the right way. It could be done, he was sure.

But his classmates were skeptical. "Princeton will never change," they told him. "The brass has always handled discipline cases this way and they always will!"

Poisoned birds littered the campus—but why be bothered? Students were expelled without a chance to appeal—but why get worked up about it?

If his classmates shrugged it off, Nader could not. Was it because, as a child, he had heard his father speak out against wrongs? Was it because he loved law and dreamed of defending people's rights in court someday? Or—probably most important—was it because the sheer power of Big Universities, Big Government, Big Business threatened to chew up the individual?

Bigness did not bother the other students. Most of them were hoping to join big oil companies, big shipping firms, big brokerage houses as soon as they left college. They saw in bigness no threat at all.

Why on earth did this Ralph Nader want to get involved, anyway?

He was graduated magna cum laude from Princeton with majors in government and economics in 1955 and the following autumn entered Harvard Law School. Attending lectures and poring over law cases in the library at Cambridge, Massachusetts, he began to investigate auto injuries and the lawsuits that resulted from them.

In one suit after another, the court assumed that if a car suddenly went out of control even when traveling at moderate speed, there was *something* wrong with the driver. (Was he emotionally upset? Inattentive? Drunk?)

If a car's transmission was labeled P N D L R, with Reverse next to Low Drive, and the driver clicked into "L" but found the car, suddenly jerking backward into a pedestrian, the *driver* was at fault.

Safety experts had warned that such a shift pattern could cause accidents. They advised carmakers to standardize it: P R N D L. This way the "N" (neutral gear) would be between Reverse and Drive. But no action had been taken. Cars continued to come off the assembly line with reverse gear adjacent to forward.

Everybody assumed it was up to the driver to be careful! As an early auto pioneer had put it, "Cars don't get people into trouble; people get cars into trouble!" This attitude was part of the folklore of Motor America. Law courts had adopted it without question.

Although his studies covered all branches of law during the three years he attended Harvard, Ralph Nader found himself coming back again and again to auto injury cases. They fascinated—and infuriated—him. Courts dealt fairly with people hurt in planes, busses, trains, ships and even on elevators. But when they rode in an automobile they were on their own. The protection of the law evaporated as mysteriously as the phantom brake fluid!

The Harvard Law Review, one of the most respected in the country, published in 1956 an article that fired Ralph's imagination. Titled "Liability of Automobile Manufacturers for Unsafe Design of Passenger Cars," it stated, "Nothing in law or logic insulates manufacturers from liability for deficiencies in design any more than for defects in construction."

If this was true, it meant that instrument panels with knife-sharp edges or knobs that protruded, bucket seats that jerked loose from floor mounts, or steering wheels that thrust back into the body of the driver in a head-on collision—all were the responsibility of the carmaker.

Nader began to piece together a profile of design hazards that could be as dangerous to the human body as engineering defects in brakes or steering. There was strong evidence that at least half of all injuries and deaths in otherwise *survivable* accidents could be traced to poorly designed car interiors.

Sgt. Elmer Paul of the Indiana state police force had originated the term "second collision" to describe these accidents. Most accident situations, he pointed out, have two stages. In the first, the car impacts a fixed barrier or another car. In the second—and this takes place a split second later—the occupants impact the car interior. The body is thrust forward or sideways, often taking a fatal bruising (as in the case of Cathy T.).

Nader also found data on exterior features that could be hazardous to pedestrians. If a car with sharp tail fins happened to roll down a slight incline at even 10 miles an hour and bump into a child, it could kill, reports pointed out.

Certain types of bumpers were also killers. Their design had a scoop effect, which could drag a pedestrian under the wheels to his death.

In his last year at Harvard Law School, Nader wrote an article for *The Harvard Law Review*, "American Cars: Designed for Death." It foreshadowed the book that was to make him famous.

Harvard awarded him a law degree ("with distinction") in 1958. He was asked to work as a research assistant to Prof. Harold Berman, an authority on Russian law, and he stayed at the Cambridge campus until leaving for six months of Army service in 1959. After discharge and a pleasure trip to Europe he opened a law office in Hartford.

For almost five years Nader practiced law in Hartford and campaigned in a small way for auto safety. But it was a discouraging business. Here and there around the country, lawyers, engineers, and doctors were also preaching the gospel of safety, either as individuals or in small groups. The multibillion-dollar auto industry answered their criticism by contending that cars were safe enough—if the driver would train himself to be careful.

"We feel our cars are quite safe and quite reliable," one executive told *The New York Times* when he was asked why the firm did not install anchors for seat belts. "The driver is the most important factor, we feel. If the drivers do everything they should there wouldn't be accidents, would there?"

This attitude could be changed, Ralph Nader decided, only if he went to Washington. There he could lobby as hard for *his* convictions as the automakers did for theirs.

About the decision he said later, "I had watched years go

by and nothing had happened. Before that, decades had gone by. I decided that what it took was total combat."

He wrote a letter to a man who was as angry about car accidents as he was—Dr. Daniel Patrick Moynihan. Moynihan, a sociologist who had served as chairman of a traffic safety committee for New York State, had recently gone to Washington as Assistant Secretary of Labor. He and Nader had corresponded about safety since they first started reading magazine articles that each was writing in the early 1960s.

Now that Nader was ready to go to Washington for "total combat" he wrote Doctor Moynihan asking for suggestions about job openings in government. Starting this way, he hoped to learn his way around Washington and launch his safety campaign gradually—without going bankrupt!

Moynihan offered a short-term assignment as consultant at the Labor Department for the fee that was standard for lawyers: $50 a working day. Nader accepted promptly.

Arriving in Washington in spring, 1964, he rented a bachelor's room in an old town house on 19th Street off Dupont Circle and reported for work. Doctor "Pat" Moynihan, a 6' 5" giant of a man, widely known for his Irish-American wit, gave the newcomer a warm welcome.

Nader was a curious mixture. His olive skin, deep-set brown eyes, and a habit of listening with fierce concentration gave him the look of an Arab scholar. But if his looks had a tinge of the Old World, his personality was hard-driving and aggressively American. He talked precisely and with punch, his long, bony hands chopping the air to emphasize a point. He laughed easily and had a healthy sense of humor. But it was obvious that he was intensely serious about his work. Studying him across the desk, Doctor Moynihan was glad Nader had come to Washington.

In ten months' work at the Labor Department Ralph Nader prepared a carefully documented 200-page study of the automobile and what might be done to make it safer. He also began to consult with the staff of the Senate Subcommittee on Executive Reorganization, which was investigating a wide range of safety problems.

The chairman was Sen. Abraham Ribicoff of Connecticut. Before coming to Washington, Ribicoff had been governor of his state and had fought vigorously against what he called "the fantastic carnage" caused by automobiles. The Connecticut highway department had cracked down on speeders and enforced strict safety measures on state roads. As a result, deaths and injuries were cut dramatically.

If lives could be saved in one state, why not in fifty? With Sen. Robert F. Kennedy of New York collaborating, the Ribicoff committee began an all-out effort to achieve this goal.

The committee staff pored over literally tons of statistics. They wanted to balance the views of carmakers against those of critics. Was it necessary, as some experts claimed, for the federal government to *regulate* the automobile? Should there be a "Federal Automobile Agency," for instance, comparable to the Federal Aviation Agency, which enforced maximum safety measures for the public when it traveled on airlines?

The idea of Washington's interfering with private industry alarmed the carmakers. They argued that the automotive industry employs, either directly or through its suppliers, more people than any other single enterprise in the world. One in every seven American workers traces his livelihood to the automobile. Its manufacture consumes 21 percent of all steel, 49 percent of all lead, and 61 percent of all rubber sold in America. To impose federal regulations would be a threat to a vital segment of the American economy, the carmakers contended.

In rebuttal, safety groups like Physicians for Automotive Safety began testifying at Ribicoff committee hearings. Doctors showed X rays of fatal skull fractures caused by the "second collision": A man had bounced upward in a car crash, hitting the "header," the steel bar reinforcing the roof. It was covered only with thin fabric—not an energy-absorbing plastic available on the market—and had killed him. A girl had been killed when she slammed forward into an instrument panel with protruding knobs. The X ray of her skull clearly showed the outline of one of the knobs.

Besides doctors, engineers also supplied information. Some of them had had years of experience staging car collisions under scientific conditions. Using new cars and dummies that are the height and weight of the average man driver, they rammed cars head on into a "fixed barrier" like a stone wall, then measured the shock on sensitive instruments taped to the dummies.

A head-on crash into a wall, pole, or other fixed barrier at only 23 miles per hour can kill riders in the front seat, it was found, unless they are "packaged" for protection—"firmly but comfortably anchored so as not to be thrown against the inside of the vehicle or ejected through it," as one report specified.

Some of the safety features engineers recommended were:

—Car seats that are anchored securely and will not wrench loose on impact.

—"Restraining devices" for the driver and passengers: lap seat belts, shoulder harness, or both.

—An auto "cabin" that is crash-resistant.

Hazards to eliminate would be the steering wheel that either thrusts backward into the body of the driver or cracks; knife-sharp edging on instrument panels; projecting knobs; door hinges or locks that fail in a crash, allowing doors to spring open.

Eliminating these dangers could save countless lives and reduce injuries dramatically, the experts declared. To prove their contention, they pointed to the pioneering work done to make airplanes progressively more crash-worthy over the years.

Hugh de Haven, who as a young man had miraculously escaped death when his two-seater plane collided in midair with another, had dedicated years to investigating a safety problem: Under what conditions can the human body survive air crashes? A fall against a surface that gives—such as sponge, foam rubber, or spring metal—can mean the difference between life and death, he found. The human body can take a tremendous amount of shock if it is "packaged" properly and if the cabin is crashworthy.

De Haven's findings were confirmed by experts at Republic Aviation and Douglas Aircraft and resulted in airplanes designed to cushion the pilot in an accident.

If it could be done with airplanes, why not with automobiles?

To get the truth, the Ribicoff committee continued interviewing a long list of informed people—both automakers and auto safety critics—among them Ralph Nader. When his assignment at the Labor Department was over, he had poured all his efforts into writing a book. Published in November, 1965, *Unsafe at Any Speed* began appearing in bookstores around the country as one carmaker after another came up to Capitol Hill to answer questions on car safety. Sales of the book zoomed and newspapers began headlining stories about "Ralph Nader, Auto Critic."

Skeptics called him a crank, a fanatic, a starry-eyed reformer. But car owners by the hundreds wrote letters thanking him for his dogged efforts.

"Why don't you look into defective tires next?" wrote a man from Colorado—and enclosed a scrap of tire from a blowout.

A judge in California sent the brake from his car and enclosed a note reading, "They've fixed it twice, and it still won't work. *You* keep it!"

A woman called from France at 4 o'clock one morning to tell him her sad experience with a foreign sports car.

How could someone 3000 miles from his room in Washington ferret out his telephone number? Nader had done everything possible to limit it to certain people in government and of the press. And the small office he rented in the National Press Building had a phone with an unlisted number. Still, people got through to him. Some reported their sad experiences with cars. Others gave him tips that would be valuable in lobbying for his cause.

Washington has some 1000 lobbyists. Many of them head offices with large staffs and make use of high-figure expense accounts to entertain lavishly at dinner and cocktail parties. They invite congressmen to a party and, during the course of the evening, swing the conversation around to their pet subject.

Ralph Nader was also a lobbyist—but without a staff and without a budget. He tapped out letters to the presidents of Ford, General Motors, Chrysler, Rolls-Royce, and Volkswagen on a secondhand portable typewriter. (Friends on Capitol Hill lent him a Mimeograph machine when he needed it.)

Working completely on his own, supporting his efforts by the royalties from his book and no other outside source of income, he launched an all-out effort, lobbying for the safety of some 60,000,000 car owners. He wrote to senators and representatives—or called them—or asked to see them at their offices. He gave them copies of a letter he had just written to Henry Ford II or George Romney, then president of American Motors. He supplied data on a steering defect he had just turned up in a technical journal.

As one congressman put it, "That Nader wouldn't let up. He overwhelmed us with facts. He wore us down!"

When a reporter asked Nader how he planned his strategy, he said, "I try to figure how to use what I have—the best form to put it in. A speech? A magazine article? A report to a congressman? A letter to a corporation? There's no formula. I use them all."

Lobbying was just as important as writing, he believed. Other books had been written on safety, some of them expertly documented. But the authors then had retired to the sidelines to wait for things to happen. Nader considered this a feeble way to tackle the automakers. Follow-through was needed. Sniping from the sidelines was not for him. He believed in facing the opposition, eyeball to eyeball.

Between his office and his room, he was working at a furious pace—seventeen or eighteen hours a day. When no trips to Capitol Hill were scheduled, he put on an old shirt, chino pants, and Army shoes to do his research.

Both the room and his office were bulging with towering stacks of technical journals and engineering statistics. The facts were there, and he was determined to keep digging them out.

An auto executive had stormed to the press, "This Nader makes irresponsible charges!"

"Not so," Nader shot back. "I can't afford to make statements without the facts to back them up!"

He had always enjoyed dinner dates with friends in government circles, but now he had no time for them. Washington is a cosmopolitan city, with restaurants offering food for every taste from East Indian curry to Russian borsch. Ralph had found an excellent restaurant that served Middle East specialties—the kind of food he had learned to love when his mother once took him to Lebanon as a child. Going to eat at this place, either alone or with friends, relaxed him. But there was no time for it now. He had to munch a quick sandwich and get back to work. A typical workday during that winter began at 6:30 or 7 A.M. and ended at 1 or 2 in the morning.

If he was working with frenzy, there was good reason. The Ribicoff hearings were drawing to a close. Congress would either approve or reject safety standards for American cars based on the committee's findings. He had to do everything possible to make his voice heard—to make an impact.

The climate was right for it, as even the carmakers began to admit. Congress had made efforts in other years to pass safety legislation. They had concentrated, though, only on superficial points. Senator Ribicoff and his staff were researching in depth. He and Senator Kennedy personally faced each witness—whatever view he held—and asked penetrating questions.

As one business magazine reported, "Even a few carmakers are giving Ribicoff's committee grudging respect. It is obvious that he is determined to get down to nuts and bolts in the safety controversy."

Trudging up to Capitol Hill through the slush that winter of 1965–66, Ralph Nader appeared countless times to report the facts he had unearthed.

Compared with the well-tailored men from Detroit driven to the hearings in their firms' limousines, he cut a strange figure. A reporter described Nader this way: "With his ragged gray tweed overcoat, his tie askew, and his long, bony hands shooting out from his rumpled suit, he looks for all the world like one of dozens of wide-eyed inventors." When he began to talk, though, he was clearly conversant with the whole field of automobile safety. He made points about too-small brake drums, front placement of fuel tanks, cars that flipped over through steering defects—all with an accuracy and a conviction that deeply impressed the committee members.

When a question was fired at him he answered immediately with statistics that could not be challenged.

Again and again he hammered home his point: The public must have a role in shaping the standards of crashworthiness in the cars it buys and from whose defects it suffers.

Studying the face of this zealous young lawyer, Sen. Robert Kennedy asked one day, "Why are you doing this?"

"If I worked for the prevention of cruelty to animals, nobody would ask me that question," he answered.

Later, when pressed to explain his motives, he said simply, "I guess I just don't like to see people taken advantage of."

"How can you criticize cars when you don't even own one?" another reporter asked.

He answered that he had nothing against the automobile itself. "They're very useful when they are safely constructed and operated. I like to drive, but it saves time and money in the city to walk or catch a cab. Besides, when I really need a car I rent one."

When the committee recessed in February, 1966, Nader left Washington for a brief trip. He had been invited to testify in Des Moines, Iowa, before a state auto safety inquiry. The pace was much slower in the Midwestern city, and the corridors in the state building were almost empty. Nader became aware that a man who seemed to have no official business at the hearing was strangely, intently interested in every move he made. When he left to go to his hotel, the man followed him briefly.

A few days later, after Nader's return to Washington, a Capitol Hill guard notified him that two men had been picked up by the police. They were private detectives hired to "tail Nader and get something on him."

In Winsted, Connecticut, it was later learned, the same two men had been asking questions about Ralph Nader's family, religion, friends, whether he had any prejudice against Jews.

A confidential folder was being prepared on him. Someone—it was not quite clear who—at General Motors had ordered it. The charge was denied by GM executives on March 9.

On March 22 Senator Ribicoff convened a special hearing to investigate whether Nader had been "harassed" for speaking out on auto safety. The hearing was televised. As millions of people watched, James M. Roche, president of General Motors, admitted that someone at the firm had ("without my knowledge") ordered a check on Nader. He agreed that there had been some harassment and apologized for it.

The effect was electrifying. Thousands of people wrote or telegraphed their congressmen demanding that they take positive action on the safety bill Nader had worked for.

"Ralph Nader's for the little man," an Illinois farmer wrote to the late Sen. Everett Dirksen. "He's not afraid to stand up for what's right. It's time we passed a safety bill!"

The National Traffic and Motor Vehicle Safety Act was passed by the Senate in June, 1966, and by the House in August. Briefly it provided for the creation of the National Traffic Safety Agency within the Department of Commerce. The head of the new agency would consult with industry, government, and university experts to establish "minimum safety standards" for new vehicles and, later, for used cars. The agency would also set minimum standards for tires.

President Johnson signed the bill into law on September 6, 1966. Standing at his side, as television cameras recorded the scene, was the young lawyer from Connecticut.

"Most of the credit for making possible this important legislation belongs to one man—Ralph Nader," editorialized the Washington *Post*. "Through his book, *Unsafe at Any Speed*, his determination, and his seemingly limitless energy, he won; a one-man lobby for the public prevailed over the Nation's most powerful industry."

"I'm a Writer of Human Comedy"

Neil Simon

Try to get a play produced on Broadway? Better forget it—the odds are one in ten million against it. Stick with what you know. You're a lucky guy—you write for the top television comedians. It's a glamorous business. And the salary's tops—$1600 a week! If you get a turn-down from this producer, put your play in the bottom drawer of your desk and forget it. How many of them have said "Yes, I'll produce it," and then changed their mind and told you no? Is it three or four in two and a half years? Stick with comedy writing, Doc. Forget the play.

Forget the play.

That was the sensible, practical thing to do. Just forget the play. Put it away in a bottom drawer of his desk at CBS in New York and relax. He had been working on it now for almost three years—working on it nights, weekends, early in the morning. When the other writers assigned to the Garry Moore television show came in to work at 10 A.M. they always found Neil Simon—"Doc"—at his typewriter. He had come in at 8 so he could get in two hours of writing on his play. He had a scene to rewrite. Or he had to invent new dialogue for a character. Or he had to change the personality of one of the characters.

Perhaps if he made all these changes, did all this rewriting, the producer who was currently holding his play might —just *might*—produce it.

But you could not be sure. How many producers had encouraged him to make changes and then, in spite of his hard work, turned him down? Was it five? Six? He was beginning to lose count.

It was a heartbreaking business—writing a play. If he gave it up, he could concentrate on doing his job—comedy writing—and then relax with his wife and baby daughter. He could sleep late in the morning and take it easy on weekends. Other top-salaried television writers relaxed on weekends by playing golf, swimming, and playing cards. After grinding out material all week for a television personality they were happy to get away from the typewriter and be lazy.

For these other television writers, the job was enough. The pace was hectic and ulcer-producing, but there were glamour and excitement in the business, and the salaries were astronomical. Simon himself had risen from $50 a week in radio to $1600 for his work on the Garry Moore Show this season of 1959–60. The year before, he had done material for Phil Silvers' *Sergeant Bilko* series. Before that it had been Sid Caesar. His credits for writing had established him as one of the brightest, fastest, funniest talents in television.

At 33, Neil Simon was at the peak of his profession. Other writers, turning out material that was sometimes funny, sometimes feeble, envied this tall, shy fellow's phenomenal ability to "pour it out." His ability to construct comic situations under pressure of deadline was a legend in television.

"With Doc Simon's talent and salary, I'd be laughing all the way to the bank!" they said.

Simon himself did not sneer at his income by any means. When Neil was sixteen his father, a salesman in New York's garment district, had urged him to get a job as a stock clerk in the district. It was hard work that paid very little and gave him no sense of pride.

"You got a strong back and you work fast—you do O.K. But you gotta sweat!" the bosses told the boys in the garment district.

By his talent and hard work Simon, while still in his twenties, had moved uptown to work in the towering skyscrapers along Madison and Fifth avenues. At this point in his life he could have decided that what he needed was not more work, more challenge, but golf lessons with a top pro —or a cruise to the Caribbean on a chartered yacht. Instead he was pouring every hour of his spare time into writing a play.

In 1958, in Hollywood on a special writing assignment for comedian Jerry Lewis, Simon had finished his material ahead of deadline and begun working on the play. The two main characters were brothers who had just moved from their parents' home in the Bronx to their first bachelor apartment in Manhattan.

To Simon, sitting at the typewriter writing the dialogue, the brothers in the play were intensely vivid—and for a good reason: He and his older brother, Danny, were the real-life models.

Doc and Danny had moved away from their parents' home and shared a Manhattan apartment in the early 1950's when they gained their first success as a team writing comedy for radio shows. The telephone calls from girls that came at the wrong time; the solid, stable Jewish father who warned his sons that they would be "bums" if they didn't settle down to conservative, middle-class life; the doting mother who worried about a cleaning woman for her sons' apartment—all were drawn from real life.

There was material here for a play—and Doc Simon was sure he could shape it into a good comedy. The title would be *Come Blow Your Horn*.

He began writing the first act in Hollywood and finished it eight weeks later after returning to New York. The first person to consider it was Herman Shumlin, one of Broadway's leading producers. It had potential, Shumlin decided —but the author would have to make several changes.

Simon agreed and started rewriting immediately. The producer read the changed script and suggested more changes. Simon did these—but still it wasn't right.

Perhaps, Shumlin told him, another producer should see it.

So he went to another. And another. And another. Each

wanted changes. The script then being circulated was the twelfth version of the original play!

One of the producers, Saint Subber, called Simon "an undisciplined George Kaufman." It was praise of a sort. George S. Kaufman, the co-author of *The Man Who Came to Dinner, You Can't Take It with You,* and a string of other smash hits, was the great comedy talent of the 1930s and '40s. Subber was saying that Neil Simon was close to his goal—but not close enough for a producer to invest $100,000 and his reputation in the play.

Another producer's verdict was much harsher: "Someday you'll write a great play. *This* isn't it!"

The turndowns were hard to take. Yet Neil Simon was professional enough to know that producers must be cautious. During each Broadway season, which extends roughly from September to June, some sixty productions arrive in New York theaters for inspection by audiences. Of these, forty—or more—will close the same season—some after giving only one performance!

There will be a few, on the other hand, that make a hit with the public and bring throngs lining up at the box office. A smash hit means good things to many people: fame to the actors, reputation to the playwright and director, and a hefty profit to the producer and the investors—or "angels" as they are called. While the play is having a sellout run on Broadway the producer may decide to set up duplicate "national" companies to tour major cities in the United States. If these prove successful, one or more companies may also be formed to play overseas, touring London, Paris, West Berlin, and perhaps going as far as Tokyo.

If a play runs for a full season, it usually repays the cost of its original investment. A long run and touring companies will make profits soar and bring wealth to the principals. The playwright, for instance, may earn $10,000 a week—or more—in royalties for his original work. Only a few writers in a decade have talent that brings such success, though. Arthur Miller was one. Tennessee Williams, William Inge, and

William Gibson are others who in recent years have achieved such a peak.

Because the rewards are so immense, countless people aspire to be the Arthur Miller or Tennessee Williams of their generation. They work months or years writing a play they are *sure* will be a smash hit. Yet it never reaches a stage. Their talent is not great enough. They lack the magic touch that creates stage characters who are believable, who take on a life of their own for three hours every night as the audience sits in a darkened theater watching them wrestle with problems tragic or funny.

Did Neil Simon have the touch? Would he be one of the rare people who pour years into a play and see it produced on Broadway? Or was he fooling himself about his talent? Every time his play was rejected he had to face these questions.

Certainly he was much closer to the goal than struggling writers turning out a play in a remote part of the country, without professional advice or criticism. He was a native New Yorker and had been working with top actors and directors for years. He had written thousands of lines of comic dialogue and knew exactly what it took to make radio and television audiences roar with laughter. Was it not logical to believe he could make *live* audiences in a theater laugh too?

The offices of the NBC and CBS networks where Simon worked are short blocks from the theaters on Broadway. It takes only a few minutes to walk from New York's Radio City to Times Square. But making the trip professionally could take how long? Another three years?

All the tension, the disappointment, the hard work would be over if he gave up. Lock the playscript away in a desk drawer and forget it. It was the prudent, practical way to end the torture he had inflicted on himself. But something wouldn't let him do it: a quiet but unquenchable conviction that he *could* take the giant step from gag writer to playwright.

His sense of humor was peculiar, was offbeat. "But I can make it work," he told his wife, "if I write about Danny and me."

Marvin Neil Simon was born on July 4, 1927, in New York's northern borough, the Bronx. There was one other child in the family, a son named Danny. Danny Simon, a fast-thinking, energetic youngster, was seven years old when his baby brother arrived. Almost as soon as little Neil started toddling, Danny began giving him the benefit of his hard-won neighborhood wisdom. The kids to play with were X, Y, and Z. The kids who would beat you up were J, K, and L.

Young Neil appreciated his brother's "savvy" in such matters, but his own interests ran in other channels. His favorite pastime was playing doctor with a toy stethoscope and he made a point of checking the heartbeat of everyone who came within range.

"Neil is a regular doctor," his mother told relatives.

"How's the doctor?" his father asked when he came home in the evening.

"Hey, Doc," Danny called, "come out and play—we need you for stickball."

"Doc" became his nickname and it remains the name his friends and business associates call him today.

In 1932, at the height of the Depression, the family moved to a section of upper Manhattan called Washington Heights and there the boys grew up. Money for entertainment had to be strictly budgeted, so listening to the radio became a regular pastime. It offered a wide range of free entertainment: daytime serials ("soap operas"), variety shows, and comedy with such stars as Fred Allen, Fibber McGee and Molly, Fanny Brice and Jack Benny.

The Simon boys listened and laughed. Laughing at comedy on radio or in the movies got to be a trademark of young Doc's. Once he was taken to an outdoor showing of a Charlie Chaplin movie.

"I climbed up on a stone ledge to watch it," he recalled

later. "I laughed so hard I fell off, cut my head open and was taken to the doctor, bleeding—and laughing. I was constantly being dragged out of movies for laughing too loud."

The actors and writers who could make a little boy laugh this hard became his idols. Years later when he was writing comedy scripts for Broadway and Hollywood he said that his idea of the "ultimate achievement in a comedy is to make a whole audience fall onto the floor, writhing and laughing. . . ."

Doc Simon was not an avid student but did manage to finish high school shortly before his seventeenth birthday. His father suggested a summer job as a stock clerk in the garment district and he worked wrestling pipe racks and packing crates during the steamy summer months of 1944.

The United States had been at war with Germany and Japan for three years and many of Doc's young friends were volunteering for service. The Air Force seemed glamorous and exciting and he joined a reserve training program.

When orders for flight training began coming through, his classmates found themselves assigned to New Mexico, Georgia, Texas—and other faraway Air Force bases. Where would Doc Simon go? everyone asked. While he was anxiously waiting for orders, his family gave him a big farewell party. A record number of friends and relatives attended, each bringing a gift.

"Then I got my orders," Simon said later. "They sent me to study basic engineering techniques at New York U.—uptown. Everybody—my mother, father, a couple of close friends, a girl friend—saw me off at the 181st Street trolley station. They said, 'Write to us.' I said I'd telephone."

Training at the uptown campus of N.Y.U. took a year, but it seemed a lot longer. "I was the only one who didn't go home on weekends. I was too ashamed."

An out-of-town assignment did finally come in August, 1945: He was sent to Lowry Field, Colorado, and took over as sports editor of the base newspaper, the *Rev-Meter*. In 1946 at the age of 19, he was discharged with the rank of corporal and came home to New York to look for work.

Danny Simon, who had been working as a publicity man in the New York office of Warner Brothers, asked one day how Doc would like to work for the picture corporation. There was an opening—in the mail room. The salary, $30 a week, was small, but there was always a chance that a bright young man like Doc would get promotions. Danny himself was making $250 a week.

The ability Danny had shown as a boy to think fast and size up people was paying handsome dividends. But he wasn't satisfied. He wanted big success—for both of them. The way to achieve it, he assured Doc, was to write for radio.

Through his contacts in show business, Danny had met men who turned out material for detective and mystery series like *Perry Mason* and *Mr. District Attorney* and for comedy shows with stars like Bob Hope and Art Linkletter. Imagine how great it would be if Danny and Doc could team up as radio writers! They'd be on their way to big money then.

To nineteen-year-old Doc working in Warner Brothers' mail room for $30 a week, Danny's ideas sounded alluring. The pair might—just *might*—be able to bring it off. Danny was a powerhouse. He generated ideas and excitement and knew dozens of important people. If he and Neil could come up with the right kind of comic material the team would be launched: Doc and Danny Simon. . . . No, that was wrong. It should be the other way around: Danny and Doc Simon.

One day after lunch, Danny rushed back to work and announced that they had their chance: Goodman Ace, a veteran radio writer who had created *Easy Aces* for CBS, was setting up a group of radio writers who would turn out comedy material on a regular workday basis. He had started auditioning and if the Simon brothers wanted to be considered for his "stable" they would have to apply immediately!

As soon as they could leave the office, they raced to CBS for an interview.

"Are you willing to try out?" Ace asked after explaining the requirements. Certainly, they told him. Ace explained that they were to do a comedy routine suitable for radio.

"What's the deadline?" Danny asked.

"Nine o'clock tomorrow morning," Ace answered.

Through most of the night they worked at a furious, brainstorming pace, pouring out ideas and dialogue, scrapping some, saving others. It was an exhausting process—but at nine o'clock the next morning they had the material for Goodman Ace.

Their character was an usherette at a Brooklyn movie theater giving her own account of a movie starring Joan Crawford. At the end the usherette says, "She's in love with a gangster who's caught and sent to Sing-Sing and gets the electric chair—and she promises to wait for him!"

Goodman Ace read it and hired them. For Doc, the venture meant a raise in salary from $30 a week to $50. For Danny, it meant a big step down. He, too, would be making only $50 a week.

But they were launched: Danny and Doc Simon were a team.

They notified Warner Brothers that the Simons were starting new creative careers elsewhere. Then they broke the news to their parents. Irving Simon was apoplectic. Danny should have known better! How could he give up $250 a week and a job with a future to work as a beginner in another field? And for $50!

"You'll be a bum all your life!" he thundered.

With Doc he was a bit easier. He grumbled and muttered reminders of the great depression. But to the two brothers, the depression was a dim memory from their boyhood days in Washington Heights. America had recovered, had fought a gigantic World War and defeated the armies of Hitler and Hirohito. There was a new confidence in the country as the first fifty years of the twentieth century drew to a close. America was strong, was stable. Manufacturers were gear-ing to turn out products for millions of military men returning home. They would be advertising on radio—and perhaps on a new gadget called television. Writers would be in demand. Danny and Doc Simon would get a chance to learn the business and grow with it.

The great, glamorous world of radio was beckoning.

Producing comedy material for radio was, as a matter of fact, not quite so glamorous as Danny and Doc had imagined. Sharing an office with several other writers—the number fluctuated, depending on who was hired and who was fired—they were ordered to grind out scripts on a strict deadline for a personality named Robert Q. Lewis. Lewis, who delivered quips in a rapid-fire, nasal tone, had a daily program on CBS radio. He consumed comedy material at an alarming rate. No matter how many writers Goodman Ace hired, and no matter how fast they worked, they always seemed at the "panic point" in their need of more material.

Danny and Doc were able to keep pace by writing at a furious clip, gulping sandwiches and coffee as they worked. But they soon began to feel that there was something unreal about their jobs. They were toiling furiously for a personality who worked somewhere in the great sprawling CBS complex. But during more than four hectic months of working for him he remained a voice and a rating. They never got to meet the flesh-and-blood Robert Q. Lewis.

When their first stint at CBS came to an end, they were given a chance to write for one of NBC's first television programs, the Phil Silvers "Arrow Show." Television comedy was scoring its first success with stars like Milton Berle, and NBC hoped that Phil Silvers would also be a hit. He proved to be only mildly successful, though, and his contract was dropped after a short run. For Danny and Doc Simon, however, the experience was valuable. Radio comedy relied strictly on oral humor. Television added another dimension —the visual. Men who were successful gag writers for radio often found it impossible to come up with comedy skits for this new medium. But the Simons were among the radio writers skillful enough to master the new medium.

As they became known in the business, assignments came from Jerry Lester, Sid Caesar, and Red Buttons. Their salaries jumped from $50 to $500 and more weekly and the brothers leased an elegant apartment.

The move saddened their parents. True, the boys had worked unbelievably hard; they wanted an apartment that reflected their success. But the departure was a wrench to Irving and Mamie Simon. When the boys lived at home there had never been a dull moment. They were two very funny fellows—Danny and Doc. Life without them would be lonely.

Many comedy writers, striving to establish themselves, found that they sometimes made useful contacts by leaving the city in the summer and going to one of the resorts frequented by TV directors, actors, and agents. The resorts in the Catskill Mountains drew many and so did some in the Pocono Mountains in Pennsylvania.

Danny and Doc favored the Poconos—Camp Tamiment, in particular. Here, in the summers of 1952 and 1953, they wrote comedy sketches for a new revue every week. The acting was done by the counselors—both boys and girls. For young people who hoped to make Broadway or Hollywood, it was a good way to create an entrée to show business.

Danny and Doc were elated at the way audiences received their revues. There was something very satisfying in writing for people and getting their reactions at firsthand. When a comedy sketch was amusing they smiled. But when it was hilarious they howled with laughter.

The brothers were training themselves in a new medium —live theater. It was possible, as several people pointed out, that they might be able to sell their revue sketches to a Broadway producer sometime in the future.

Whether their sketches sold or not, they still considered

their working vacations a success. They were having a wonderful time and both brothers had met girls they wanted to marry. Doc Simon's girl was a pretty young dancer, Joan Baim, who was a counselor in the Tamiment girls' camp.

The marriages of both brothers broke up their bachelor apartment. Doc and Joan Simon found an apartment on the top floor of an ancient building on East Tenth Street in Greenwich Village. Prominent in the ceiling was a skylight with glass that had ruptured away from the frame. Sleeping on a couch in the living room one winter night, Doc found snow sifting down on his face. So many things went wrong with the little apartment that it seemed to develop a perverse personality of its own. He had never lived in any place quite like it. It left an indelible impression.

In 1955, when the Simon brothers had been working as a team for more than seven years, they sold their first scripts to a Broadway producer for a revue called *Catch a Star!* The comedy sketches were some they had created originally for Tamiment and rewritten for the stage. *Catch a Star!* ran for only twenty-three performances. Building on this experience, though, they turned out new sketches and sold them the following year to *New Faces of 1956*, which had a moderate success with 220 performances.

The hard, grinding business of writing television comedy under harsh deadlines was beginning to pall on Danny Simon. He wanted a change and in 1956 left New York to try his skill as a television director on the West Coast. For the first time in his career Doc Simon began writing completely on his own.

Television had become so popular by the mid-1950s that stars like Ed Sullivan, Lucille Ball, and Sid Caesar and Imogene Coca were displacing movie stars as favorites with the American public.

Entertainers usually favored one of two types of formats. The first was the variety show, which had been pioneered by Milton Berle in the late 1940s. It was built around an entertainer like Berle, who appeared in comedy sketches and also served as a master of ceremonies to introduce other performers. This was the format that later served so well for Jackie Gleason, George Gobel, Sid Caesar, Red Skelton, and a host of others.

The second type was the situation comedy series, popularized by *I Love Lucy* in the early 1950s; it won such immediate success that it, too, became a standard. Each season several new situation comedies were launched: *Father Knows Best, Ozzie and Harriet, Leave It to Beaver, Sergeant Bilko,* and dozens of others won loyal fans.

As television became firmly established as an entertainment medium that was important to advertisers and popular with the public, some facts about it became obvious. It had evolved from radio and had much in common with the older medium: It was a communications pipeline to the public, broadcasting news and entertainment free of charge to anyone who bought a receiver.

But television made much greater demands on creative people than radio. A career in radio could span fifteen years or more as Jack Benny, George Burns, Fred Allen, and others proved.

Just the opposite was true in TV, though. When the American public saw a star's face week after week on the screen they often became tired of his image and switched channels. Then ratings went down. When this happened the advertiser became unhappy, network officials began to worry, and new ideas and new routines were loudly called for.

Writers who could not generate a constant stream of usable material were fired. Taking their place were others who might last a whole season or one week. Danny and Doc Simon had experienced this kind of revolving-door employment a few times, even though they were established writers. They worked on the Jackie Gleason Show for a single week. And they wrote briefly for Red Buttons—two of 163 writers he hired in two seasons!

The pressure of creating a clever new show every seven days drained the energies of stars and writers. Everyone assigned to it raced the clock—scripts had to be pounded out at a furious pace, approved by the comedian, rushed to the typing pool, and then put into production on the rehearsal stage while the director blocked out cues for the camera crew.

Men able to write under these conditions were highly paid. Doc Simon earned $1,600 a week writing for Phil Silvers's *Sergeant Bilko* series and the Garry Moore variety show, but he found little satisfaction in it.

"It was very tedious," he said later. "It's degrading to try to be funny when you don't feel like it."

Often in the evening when he and his wife were watching a television program Joan would laugh and say, "That's a funny line—I bet *you* wrote that."

Had he written it? He wasn't sure. He had been closeted in an office with six or seven other writers, all of them spouting gags as fast as they could. The ones actually created by Doc Simon were hard to identify—they fused into the great mass almost the instant they were generated.

Fortunately not all television writers worked with such a feeling of futility. Those lucky enough to write full-length dramatic shows found that the TV medium gave full scope to their talents. Authors like Paddy Chayefsky, Robert Alan Aurthur, Reginald Rose, and William Gibson wrote hour-long dramas that won large audiences. More important, TV dramatic scripts that had special appeal, like Chayefsky's *Marty* and Gibson's *The Miracle Worker,* could be adapted for the theater, movies, or both.

These writers were the lucky ones. They didn't have to grind out comedy scripts on order. They had escaped what comedian Fred Allen once called the "treadmill to oblivion."

Doc greatly admired these writers who had made the switch from television to the theater. He began to read books on playwriting and signed up for playwriting courses. He soon discovered, though, that they could supply technique—but not talent. "The trouble is they teach you to write the way *other* people do," he told his wife.

George S. Kaufman, Garson Kanin, John Van Druten, George Abbott—all had written marvelous comedies, but their thinking was different, their styles were different from his. Copying them would be useless. Doc had to hammer out his own craftwork for the theater. He had written thousands of lines of comic dialogue. He knew how to make radio and television audiences roar with laughter. But a full-length play takes much more. It must have vivid characters and strong situations that will trap the attention of the audience in Act One and hold it until the final curtain.

Vivid characters . . . strong situations. He was sure the play he had in mind had these two essential ingredients.

In the summer of 1958, comedian Jerry Lewis asked him to go to the West Coast on a special assignment. "You should be able to finish it in five weeks," Lewis told him.

Simon had been pouring out comedy material for so many comics for so many years that he was able to complete the Jerry Lewis assignment in just one week. With time to kill and only an occasional conference to keep him busy, another writer might have headed for the golf course. But the play that had been building in Neil Simon's mind for so long wouldn't give him any peace. He sat down at the typewriter one morning and began work on Act One of the play, calling it *Come Blow Your Horn*. When he flew back to New York a month later the characters were beginning to take shape vividly in his mind.

Two months later it was finished. Crossing his fingers for luck, he sent it off to a Broadway theater producer—and thus became enmeshed in a process that was to last three years and involve almost as many challenges as Jason's quest for the Golden Fleece.

The first producer to read it was impressed. Good potential, he said, but it needs changes. Doc made them eagerly. But the new version of his play did not please the producer as much as the first version. What had happened? The producer could not put his finger on it. Perhaps the author would do better if he took it to another producer.

The next man liked it immensely, signed a contract to produce it, but found he could not interest enough backers to raise sufficient money.

It was then taken to Saint Subber, the producer who called him an "undisciplined George Kaufman"—but also rejected the script.

When it reached the office of David Merrick, a Broadway tycoon who is famous for finding talent, Simon was sure the waiting and the disappointments were over. Merrick liked it immensely and said he would produce it if a good comedy director like Garson Kanin would direct it.

Simon told him that Kanin had seen it through another producer—but turned it down.

Merrick was still interested. "I'll produce it if Joshua Logan will direct."

Simon told him that Logan had turned it down too.

"I'll produce it if George Abbott will direct," Merrick replied.

Abbott also had turned it down.

Merrick shrugged. "So I'm turning it down too!"

Inching up to success only to have it snatched away at the last minute was maddening. Eight producers had read his play and sent it back. Why not stop torturing himself? Why not put it away in a desk drawer and forget it?

In desperation he called Michael Ellis, manager of the Bucks County Playhouse, a summer theater in New Hope, Pennsylvania. Would Ellis consider it for his 1960 stock season? Doc just wanted to see it on a stage—any stage. He had hoped for Broadway—but Bucks County would do.

Ellis read it and decided that it was light enough and funny enough for summer audiences. But it needed a few changes. . . .

Simon took a deep breath and went doggedly back to his

typewriter. In thirteen years of writing for radio and television and the three years writing the play, he had developed superhuman patience.

A sign announcing *"Come Blow Your Horn,* a new play by Neil Simon," went up outside the Bucks County Playhouse. In August, when the curtain finally went up—on the fifteenth version—and the story began to unfold, audiences roared with laughter. The characters that Simon had created—a strong-minded Jewish father and his equally strong-minded sons—did come to life on the stage. Vivid characters and strong situations, the two essentials, were evident in this play. Doc Simon had the touch.

Michael Ellis was delighted. "Let's do it on Broadway!" he told the playwright.

With William Hammerstein and Ellis as co-producers, it came to Broadway—in its sixteenth version—the following winter, opening at the Plymouth Theater on Washington's Birthday, 1961. Some critics were kind, some found fault with it. But there were people at the box office the next day and slowly it built to a moderate success over its run of 85 weeks.

Lou Jacobi, who acted the role of the father, a manufacturer of artificial fruit, became a special favorite with audiences. Simon had based the character on his own father—a man who stood up to his strong-minded sons when he thought they were headed in the wrong direction.

"You're a bum!" the father thunders at his stage son—just as Irving Simon had once thundered at Danny Simon.

One evening when Irving Simon saw the play he turned to a friend and whispered, "I *know* people like that!"

The character as created by Simon had warmth and appeal that went far beyond Jewish middle class. Simon was sitting in a back row watching audience reaction one matinee when he saw the elderly Negro porter employed by the Plymouth Theater howling with laughter.

"You've seen the play at least forty times. What's so funny?" he asked the man.

"That's *my* father," came the answer.

When *Come Blow Your Horn* settled down to a steady run, an offer came from Hollywood—$250,000 for the film rights. Simon accepted and leased a small office on 57th Street.

"Now I can afford the luxury of playwriting," he said.

He had finally escaped the routine of television writing. But he decided to keep to the work habits he had practiced so long. When he's working on a play he reports for work at his office at 10 o'clock and often writes steadily until five or later, sipping coffee or milk and munching dry roasted peanuts.

"Does it ever get boring?" a reporter asked.

"Never," he answered. "I once worked in the garment district lifting heavy things. Now I sit here in my office doing what I like. Writers who complain about how hard it is just don't like writing!"

His work routine is so successful and his output so large that he has been able to turn out almost one hit a year since his first success.

Little Me, a musical fantasy starring Sid Caesar, opened in 1962 and ran for 223 performances. The following year he finished *Barefoot in the Park* and New York critics praised it generously.

One declared, "If there is an empty seat at the Biltmore Theater for the next three years, it will be because someone has just fallen out of it—laughing at Neil Simon's new comedy."

The story concerns a stuffy young lawyer and his free-spirited bride and their troubles in an ancient apartment with cold radiators and a leaky skylight. The apartment was modeled, of course, on the one he and his wife, Joan, rented on East Tenth Street in Greenwich Village when they were first married.

Corie, the young bride in the play who wants to go walking barefoot in the park, and Paul, the conservative young husband, have unusual neighbors: an impulsive Hungarian who cooks exotic dishes and occasionally darts along the roof, and another tenant on a lower floor who is never seen but puts out nine empty cans of tuna in the hall every day. (Could it be a giant cat with a can opener? Paul wonders.)

Barefoot in the Park, also bought for the movies, was destined to run for 1532 performances over four years. During this time Neil Simon wrote *The Odd Couple*, *The Star-Spangled Girl*, and adapted *Sweet Charity*. For a brief period all four were running simultaneously on Broadway—bringing him royalties as high as $20,000 a week.

When his *Plaza Suite* opened in 1968 and became an immediate sellout, an associate remarked that he was overextending himself.

"Not so," countered a friend from television days. "His output is tremendous. It just pours out of him. He can write a play every year for 25 years."

He has also had to face the charge that he writes only "commercial" plays. To this he answers: "Comedy happens to be the most difficult thing to pull off well—and the most prone to be knocked. Writing comedy has to come out of enormous confidence. You have to say to a theater audience, 'Listen, 900 people, this is funny!' "

Veteran actors and producers who have followed Neil Simon's amazing success since his first breakthrough on Broadway feel that he appeals to millions of people for two reasons. First, he sticks closely to everyday situations.

"He is not far-out, not zany," says Mike Nichols, who directed *Barefoot in the Park* and *The Odd Couple*.

The funny lines his characters speak come out of situations that could happen to almost anyone. In *The Odd Couple*, Felix, after a quarrel with his wife, moves in with Oscar, recently divorced. Oscar is worried about Felix's mood of depression but finally shrugs it off. "He's too nervous to kill himself," he says. "He wears his seat belt in a drive-in theater."

The second reason for Neil Simon's appeal is that his humor has heart.

"One important thing I've learned about comedy," he

once said, "is to make your characters likable even when you're exposing their worst faults."

The father in *Come Blow Your Horn* storms at his sons—and the older one storms back. Yet, as Neil Simon wrote the characters, the family's squabbles did not basically change the devotion each generation felt for the other.

Paul and Corie stamp and snarl, but the audience knows that they will eventually work out the snags in their marriage because they love each other deeply.

In *The Odd Couple* Felix and Oscar have both failed as husbands. Yet Felix never blames his wife for the breakup or speaks slightingly of his children—he shows their pictures even to strangers. Oscar, the other central character, is something of a cynic, but he can be loyal and generous to friends.

Danny Simon, who for years tried to convince people that his shy younger brother was loaded with talent, is especially proud of Doc's million-dollar-a-year success. The secret, he says, is that Doc "tries to focus only on the smaller problems of the people he knows. That's why audiences love the characters in his plays. They're written with love and sympathy."

One question that reporters almost always ask the big, genial man is this: "Would you ever like to write a serious play?"

"Why should Willie Mays become a football player?" he once countered. "Why should I write dull serious plays? I know it sounds pretentious, but I'm a writer of human comedy. For myself, there's nothing more important. The thing to do is to make them more and more human."

For years when he was working as a gag writer in television, Neil had a recurring dream: People take their seats in a theater, the lights dim, the curtain goes up, and on the stage, actors begin to talk and move as the story unfolds. It's a funny story and the audience rocks with laughter. But it is not slapstick, not a farce. There are serious moments in the play too. It is humor with heart.

He knew he could write this way, could be more than a

highly paid gag writer. But it took three years of turndowns to prove it. Again and again he had to hear, "Yes-we-will-produce-it-no-we-won't." But Neil Simon does not give up easily. He is a soft-spoken man with dogged determination. He was sure that if he could get past the men saying "No" he could get to people in the theaters—and they would say "Yes" by the millions.

"In Advertising, Make Waves— Not Ripples"

Mary Wells

It was sultry in Youngstown, Ohio, that afternoon in August, 1949, and the buyers' office in the department-store basement was almost unbearably hot.

At a scarred desk cluttered with fabric samples and newspaper layouts, the basement manager sat reading an ad. Beside him, a slim young girl stood motionless, watching his eyes scan the lines of ad copy she had composed so laboriously.

"No!" he said, thrusting the paper at her. "It's not what I want. Forget adjectives, Mary! This isn't Neiman-Marcus. Just stick to the facts. It's a sale on wash dresses. And be sure 'SALE' is all caps—and big type!"

Mary Berg took the ad and walked slowly back to her desk in the far corner. *Forget adjectives. Be sure "SALE" is in big type. This isn't Neiman-Marcus. . . .*

She looked around the dimly lighted basement with its counters piled with cotton shirts and blue jeans. The boss was right. This wasn't Neiman-Marcus!

It was a plain, very ordinary store with a firm belief in old-fashioned selling practices: Merchandise was displayed conservatively (the dummies in the store windows had prim and proper faces) and merchandise was advertised conservatively. This was the way to appeal to the customers who had been coming to the store for years.

Youngstowners were not used to opening their newspapers at night and reading ads that were sparkling or different. They expected to see "SALE!" in big type, and the basement manager was not one to disappoint them.

Mary knew all these things about the store, yet she was grateful to be working there. She was young and inexperienced and wanted desperately to learn advertising. It was a good place to start.

She had been hired early that summer. ("As long as you can type we'll give you a trial," the boss said.) In the first few weeks she met the bosses, the buyers, and the salespeople, and began to learn some of the basics of merchandising.

A department store, even a small one like this, was a complex organism that required the meshing of many talents. Mary really had much to offer. She knew Youngstown—she had been born there twenty-one years before and had spent summers there when her classes at Carnegie Tech ended each year in June.

She also knew the general basics of selling. Her father, Waldemar Berg, was a furniture company salesman and in the years when she was growing up she had unconsciously absorbed his principles of appealing to the public.

Millions of people all over the United States go shopping in department stores for boots, bicycles, refrigerators, and clothing. Why do they flock to some stores and not others? What is the appeal—in fashion, for instance—that makes some stores world-famous? What makes Neiman-Marcus unique? Or Macy's? And what part does advertising play in their success?

These were questions that fascinated Mary and drew her to advertising. Good ads influence people to act in certain ways. The person who knows how to create them can go to the top in the advertising field. Mary was sure of it. It made working in the bargain basement that sweltering summer bearable.

At night when she went home she brought ads the store was running in Youngstown newspapers and analyzed them. Mary had spent two years of fashion study at Carnegie Tech. She knew when something appealed and when it fell flat. If she had had a free hand to work on those store ads they might have had "pizazz."

It was worth dreaming about—and working toward. When she left Carnegie, Mary planned to go either to Chicago or to New York. She was sure she could make a name for herself in advertising once she got to a big city.

For that sticky summer of 1949, meanwhile, there was routine ad writing to be done at a beginner's salary.

SALE! Summer clearance on boys' shirts.

SALE! Ladies' swimsuits at big savings.

SALE! Boys' blue jeans—all sizes, slim to husky.

On days when Mary's morale needed a lift she called her mother and made a lunch date. Just a sandwich and iced tea with brisk Mrs. Berg could bring her out of the doldrums.

"Everything will work out," she would assure Mary. "You're learning the basics of advertising—that's the important thing. And what you learn now in a little job you'll be able to use in a big one someday."

Learn. It was the watchword of Violet Berg's life. She had begun instilling the idea of study and self-improvement in her only child when Mary was a girl of five. Mary had been invited to a birthday party. While all the other children played games, chattered, and giggled, Mary stood silently watching them. She wanted to be part of the fun but was too shy.

It pained Mrs. Berg to see her on the sidelines. Something had to be done to give this child confidence.

Mary Georgene Berg had been blessed with good brains, good health, and good looks. She had soft, ash-blond hair, clear brown eyes, and delicate features. She was an appealing child with only one handicap: shyness. This certainly could be helped, Mrs. Berg decided. She would start by having her daughter take lessons in "self-expression" with an elocution teacher.

Mary learned to read and recite short poems and stories —some of them dramatic, others funny—for friends at small recitals. She was an eager student and each time she gave a recitation she gained confidence.

Mrs. Berg's remedy worked so well for Mary that she prescribed regular doses of dramatics and music (including lessons on the drums!) all during Mary's grammar and high-school days. By the time she graduated from high school Mary had appeared in so many amateur and semiprofessional plays in Youngstown that she was completely at ease in front of an audience.

The next logical step seemed to be training at a first-rate professional dramatics school. When Mary was seventeen Mrs. Berg brought her to New York to enroll her as a student in the Neighborhood Playhouse School of the Theater.

Mary was impressed more by New York than by dramatics. When her first year's course was up she informed her parents that what she would really like to do was train for a career in merchandising. She picked Carnegie Institute of Technology in Pittsburgh and started studying there in 1948.

It was on the Carnegie campus that she met Burt Wells, a student of industrial design. They dated steadily during Mary's second year and were married three days after Christmas, 1949.

The following June, Burt graduated and he and Mary left for New York. They had supercharged energy, ambition, and talent. Enough talent to go to the top in their field? Enough to compete with all the ambitious young men and women who come from Boise, Des Moines, Natchez, Phoenix and other towns in America and converge on New York every year looking for career success?

Mary had been testing herself—first with her mother's prodding, then with her own—since she was five years old. She arrived in New York with quiet confidence. She was sure she could go to the top.

With only her summer job—writing ads in Youngstown—to offer as experience, she applied to Macy's, the world's largest store, and was accepted. There was something about this girl with the beautiful ash-blond hair and soft voice that was different—that commanded respect.

Again, as at the Youngstown department store, she met buyers, managers, salespeople—but Macy's had hundreds of specialists on its huge staff. Each had a point of view about advertising and what Macy's ad staff should say about Christmas toys, art needlework, luggage, diamonds, cosmetics, or carpeting.

Ad writing at the Youngstown store was like dabbling a toe in a duck pond. Ad writing at the mammoth store on New York's Broadway at Thirty-fourth Street was like swimming in the Atlantic in a pounding surf. It was an exhilarating—if sometimes bruising—experience!

Retail advertising—the kind a store does when it takes space in a local newspaper to announce that certain merchandise is offered to the public for x amount of dollars—can be composed either by an ad agency or by the advertising staff at the store itself. Large department stores around the country almost without exception have their own staffs of artists and writers to design the ads and place them in the papers. Store officials then watch closely to see how certain ads "pull." If young men's blazers are on special sale and the store places a good-sized ad announcing this fact, store executives want to see exactly how many customers come to buy blazers.

If the ad does not pull very well, perhaps the artist's picture was poor or the writer's description was fuzzy. Good artists and talented copywriters have an instinct for presenting young men's blazers—or slipcovers or television sets—in ads that will pull strongly. And it was soon apparent that Mary Wells was one of these young copywriters. In the two years she worked at Macy's, she learned to analyze women's fashions and to spot trends so unerringly that she could sit down at a typewriter and translate her ideas into ad copy that had whopping pull. She knew how to describe a swimming suit, an evening dress, a new spring coat so appealingly that women reading her description beat a path to Macy's to buy it.

By the time she was 23, Mary was fashion advertising

manager of Macy's and was known for her fashion flair and hard work. She began to get offers from other stores and also from advertising agencies. One of them, from McCann-Erickson, was especially tempting and she joined the firm when she was 24. She had landed her first job on Madison Avenue.

Working at an agency meant that Mary had to learn a whole new approach to advertising. A department store created ads for itself and placed them usually in only one "medium"—newspapers—in the 1950s. An agency, on the other hand, creates ads for many different businesses which it calls "clients" and then places them in many media—newspapers, magazines, television, radio, billboards.

An ad agency in Los Angeles, New York, or any other good-sized city in the country often handles advertising accounts that are widely varied. Their clients may include an airline, a new brand of packaged soups, cosmetics, a bank, a soft drink, a European sports car, and—as a public service—a city health department ("Starve a rat today!").

The agency head assigns certain staff people to work on one or two "accounts" at a time. If their assignment is the soft drink, for example, they must find out everything they can about the product—its strong points, the competitive problems it may be having with other colas in the area, and the probable "consumer": Is this a soft drink that will appeal to children and grownups or just grownups? What should the bottle look like? What colors and wording should go on the six-pack container, and finally—how should it be promoted: with newspaper ads, on billboards, on television? Or perhaps with some combination of these?

When the marketing and research specialists at an agency come up with satisfactory answers to these questions the creative staff—copywriters and artists—can start generating ideas. They will carefully plan an overall campaign and then explain it to the cola officials at a "presentation."

Their proposed campaign may be geared to a cartoon

character, for instance, an appealing dwarf who will become identified with the product. He would appear in all newspaper and billboard ads and would be presented in one-minute cartoon "spots" on television. (Artists who specialize in "animation" techniques prepare these spots following a script that has been prepared by copywriters. The dwarf's voice is "dubbed in" by an actor. Finally background music that is catchy and humable is composed and recorded.)

All these proposals for the "dwarf" campaign are outlined in great detail at the presentation. The cola officials listen critically and ask penetrating questions. If they are satisfied that the general public will like it and will buy their product they sign a contract with the agency.

Now all departments at the agency move into high gear. The "time" buyers begin arranging with television networks and local stations to show the cola cartoon spot to the TV audience. They recommend, for instance, that it be shown five mornings a week immediately after the news and on Friday nights during an intermission of the "Comedy Movie."

They buy time on the networks, and the cola dwarf is beamed out to TV screens in millions of homes across the country. To both the cola company and the ad agency this launching of a campaign is as full of suspense as a space launching is to a scientist. If the agency has done its job well, the campaign will develop enough "thrust" to send it into orbit. If not, it will fizzle out and end up "down range."

As millions of Americans watch the cola dwarf on TV screens they decide, often subconsciously, to buy or not to buy the product. If they buy—and sales climb—the ad agency has a solid success to its credit.

Advertising agency work is complex and demanding. The young person who goes into it must be able to work under pressure, to generate original ideas, and to meet deadlines. Mary had faced the same challenges in the two years she worked at Macy's. But she had been limited to fashion advertising that was directed to newspaper readers only. At McCann-Erickson she had to tailor her writing to magazines, radio, TV, and all media—and to a wide range of products.

Mary began to mesh her writing skills with those of the most talented artists and photographers in New York. This was the exciting, glamorous part of the ad business. But she was not satisfied with being just a skilled copywriter; she wanted to learn everything about the field: how products are styled or restyled to make them appealing; how well-designed cardboard displays or posters in a store can influence people to buy quickly then and there; how to weigh the cost of advertising in a magazine against advertising on radio or TV; how to study an ordinary product so intensively that you come up with one very special thing about it that had been overlooked by all other ad people—and even the manufacturer himself!

Mary set out to master all branches of advertising and in the five years she was at McCann-Erickson she achieved her goal.

In 1957, to broaden her experience, she took a job with Doyle Dane Bernbach, an agency that was generally regarded by people in advertising as one of the most stimulating and creative anywhere in the world.

Many products are advertised as "the best . . ." or "the fastest . . ." or "the newest. . . ." The creative thinkers at Doyle Dane Bernbach did not believe in piling on adjectives. "We don't outshout the competition," soft-spoken William Bernbach told his copywriters. He advised them to take a low-key, humorous approach instead.

Two of the clients at Doyle Dane were Avis car rentals and Volkswagen. Humor had paid off handsomely for both. Avis ads were geared to the slogan "We're Only No. 2—We Try Harder!" and buttons with this slogan appeared on coat lapels and children's book bags all over the country. For Volkswagen the slogan was "Think Small," and it made a strong impression wherever it was shown.

Mary found the creative climate at Doyle Dane immensely stimulating. The people on its staff were skilled professionals who firmly believed in motivating people to buy a product—instead of nagging them to buy it.

"Be sure you put 'SALE' in big type and all caps," her boss had told Mary years before in Youngstown. That was the old-fashioned pound-it-in, "hard sell" type of advertising. The newer way to sell goods and services assumed that the public had intelligence and sensitivity.

"People want to look at a magazine ad or a television commercial and chuckle," was the way William Bernbach explained it.

To Mary Wells it sounded like something she had been waiting to hear all her life!

Doyle Dane Bernbach was different in another important way. At other ad agencies there were always a few people who considered that they were wasting their talents—they should be writing a great novel instead of word descriptions of consumer products. This, however, was a different kind of "shop."

"There are no aspiring novelists hiding out at Doyle Dane," Mary told a friend. "The atmosphere is 'hard work.' Their only concern is producing great advertising."

The job fitted her talents and ambitions so well that she quickly made a reputation for being a writer of real flair and brilliance. Promotion followed promotion and she was finally named a vice-president and associate copy chief in 1963, with a salary reputed to be $40,000.

As one of the top executives of a trend-setting agency, she was concerned with originating ideas for clients. General Mills, for instance, had a contract with Doyle Dane Bernbach to advertise its cereals. It occurred to Mary that they could do a real service for homemakers by bringing out a quality line of package dinners: casserole meals that could be easily prepared. Executives at General Mills liked her idea and went to work mass-producing them for supermarkets

and food stores. (Mary and Burt Wells had adopted two little girls and when Mary talked to a manufacturer about any
product that concerned children her opinions were firmly
rooted in her own experience.)

Persuading executives of some of America's biggest companies to market a new line of goods or adopt a radically
new approach in advertising is a tough challenge. When
they sit down with agency people at a presentation, for instance, and listen to recommendations on how to spend
money—perhaps millions—to advertise their product they
ask hard questions:

What proof do you have that the public will try our
brand?

Isn't this campaign—or aren't these TV commercials—a
little *too* funny? We want the public to chuckle *with* us—
but not laugh *at* us!

To answer tough questions from the client the agency always sends out staff people who are experts at communicat-
ing ideas. Mary became one of these for Doyle Dane
Bernbach. Her background qualified her to explain an ad
campaign so well that even the most skeptical business executives were usually convinced.

When she stood up to talk to a packed meeting of business executives, she was breezy and articulate but never
shrill. Training in diction and voice projection and the dramatic lessons she had taken were all paying dividends: She
had a soft, appealing voice and a simple way of communi-
cating ideas—almost as if she were talking on a one-to-one
basis with every person in the room.

"She gets their attention so completely in the first five
minutes that they listen hypnotically," one man reported.

Even people from rival ad agencies called her "absolutely
devastating" at a business meeting.

"All the lessons—the elocution and dramatics—are paying
off," she wrote her mother. "If I'm a success, it's because you
expected me to be one."

Some career women who watched her spectacular rise

began to say enviously that she was bound to succeed; she had many things in her favor: good looks, years of voice and dramatic training, and cool, sure poise when she made a presentation to a group of executives.

Mary Wells, who was working incredibly long hours perfecting her ideas, was impatient with the notion that looks alone can bring success.

"If sales go up," she retorted, "the client doesn't care if you have green feathers and Swiss-cheese ears."

Every year she spent at Doyle Dane Bernbach brought offers from other agencies, offers that were hard to resist. Finally in 1964 she was approached by executives of a new firm: Jack Tinker and Partners. They were setting up shop in a penthouse and planned to approach advertising problems in a unique way. There would be no "copywriters" or "artists" or "researchers." Instead, the agency would draw together people from all these backgrounds and put them to work generating ideas as freely as possible.

"We're not going to be bound by traditional approaches," they explained. "We'll solve problems in the best way—even if it's never been done that way before."

Rumors of the new experimental agency spread rapidly and critics began calling it a "think factory" or a "think tank." The nicknames didn't bother people going to work for Tinker, however. The concept behind it was too exciting and the salaries were too tempting.

In 1964 Mary Wells was asked to join the creative staff at Tinker. She was 36 years old and had been with Doyle Dane Bernbach for seven profitable years. But the new offer was irresistible: She would have a great measure of freedom to experiment—and a salary of $60,000 a year.

One of the first clients to bring its problems to the penthouse staff was Miles Laboratories. Sales of their Alka-Seltzer had dipped and they wanted to reverse the trend.

Two young men were called in on the account: Richard Rich, a writer, and Stewart Greene, an artist. They convinced Miles executives that "Speedy," the little cartoon character used by the company for many years, should be retired. In his place they devised a series of TV commercials that quickly won the public's favor: shots of stomachs that wiggled, vibrated, and bounced to music but could be soothed by Alka-Seltzer. ("No matter what shape your stomach's in. . . .")

Sales began to climb and the client was delighted.

The next advertiser had an even more serious problem. It was a small airline based in Texas—Braniff International. Braniff's president, a handsome, energetic executive named Harding Lawrence, had talked with several ad agencies about his firm's problems. They carried passengers and cargo in the Midwest and to Latin America principally but weren't well known outside those areas. Lawrence was worried about the future of his line. Did it have enough aggressive thrust to compete with the giants?

One ad agency after another advised Braniff to make a survey "to define what your public image is." Harding Lawrence considered this a waste of time and money. The public image of Braniff was that of a huff-and-puff airline which hopped from one dusty town in the Southwest to another—sometimes on schedule! Braniff did not need another survey to define its image. It needed an aggressive, exciting new campaign to change that image.

Lawrence found it at Jack Tinker and Partners in the person of Mary Wells. Almost at once she saw the problem and began generating ideas. To help, she called in the two men who had been so successful with the Alka-Seltzer campaign, Richard Rich and Stewart Greene.

The three agreed that Braniff's theme could be "The end of the plain plane." An artist who specialized in color for industry was called in as a consultant and was asked, "How can we restyle Braniff planes so that they'll be noticed on landing fields even though they're outnumbered by TWA, American, Pan-Am, and all the other giants?"

"Repaint them," he advised. "They don't all have to be silver. Every airline has silver planes and they tend to make monotonous patterns on the runway. If you want the public to notice Braniff planes, paint each a different color."

But this was only the beginning. Color ideas could work for passenger lounges and even ticket counters. And Braniff stewardesses could scrap their conservative uniforms for outfits that would make fashion news. Why not get a top designer like Emilio Pucci to design trend-setting clothes for Braniff stewardesses?

"The end of the plain plane" theme was beginning to snowball.

When Harding Lawrence was told the new ideas he gave cautious approval. But the other executives of Braniff International also had to give their sanction and they were conservative businessmen who knew little about making a smashing effect in advertising. A presentation was arranged so that Mary could explain exactly how the Tinker agency proposed to use bold techniques to lift Braniff into national prominence.

Almost all ad people when they give presentations make use of expensive audio-visual aids: movie projectors, film clips, slides, tapes, records, graphs, and charts. When Mary went to the Braniff executives to present her campaign ideas, however, she planned to make it as simple as possible. She walked in with a few sketches of the planes as they would look when repainted—and colored toy blocks to show how they would appear on the runway. When she got up to speak it was obvious, though, that she did not need elaborate gimmicks. She explained her ideas simply yet so warmly that the Braniff management gave its enthusiastic approval.

Word was flashed triumphantly back to the Tinker staff at the penthouse: "Braniff bought the whole package."

Contracts were signed and work was begun immediately on the Pucci costumes and on redecorating the planes inside and out. As the target date—January, 1966—approached, both the airline and the Tinker agency throbbed with hard work.

Agency people all along Madison Avenue and executives of rival airlines were watching the experiment closely and critically. At lunch tables in New York's smart restaurants there were snide remarks about "the girl who's painting the planes," and "the Easter-egg airline."

The remarks reached the ears of Harding Lawrence and he began to have misgivings. "Are you *sure* you can bring this off?" he asked Mary bluntly. She told him she was positive.

"All right," he answered, "if this is the way you want it, this is the way it will be!"

The campaign keyed to "the end of the plain plane" was launched on schedule, and it was apparent from the start that its goal to "create excitement" had been achieved. Travelers reading ads that said, "We don't get you there any faster—it just seems that way!" were amused by this honest and offbeat approach. They talked to friends and business associates about it, and Braniff planes began filling up on runs to the Southwest. In addition, firms doing business in Mexico and South America began sending a record volume of goods on Braniff cargo planes. Sales went up 115 percent and profits climbed 41 percent.

Congratulations poured in for all the people who had worked on the campaign. The lion's share of the credit, however, went to Mary. Her "color explosion" idea jolted the public into noticing and patronizing an airline they had long ignored. Even advertising people who had scoffed had to admit that Mary Wells was a brilliant innovator.

The executives at Jack Tinker and Partners had raised Mary's salary to $80,000 a year. Now they asked her to sign a long-term contract. It was a dream offer and there were solid reasons why she should accept it. She had been divorced the year before. As a parent with two daughters to rear she was naturally concerned about financial returns for her talents.

Yet, thinking ahead, she could not picture herself staying with Tinker on a long-term basis. They were growing rapidly, adding important new clients, but as they grew they were losing some of their freedom to experiment. This was important to Mary: She was an innovator and she had to work in an atmosphere that encouraged innovation.

One day in late March, 1966, she came to a decision: She resigned her position at Tinker. The following day, Richard Rich and Stewart Greene resigned also. Whatever the three did in the future they wanted to do as a team, not individually.

Job offers began pouring in and they met at Mary's apartment one afternoon to compare prospects. It was here that Rich made a casual proposal. "We could," he said, "always open our own agency."

It seemed the perfectly logical next step. Opening an advertising agency is a risky business. But all three were trend setters whose teamwork in the past had been strikingly successful. There was every reason to believe that by pooling their talents in their own agency they could make a solid success in the future.

That afternoon the firm of Wells, Rich, Greene became a reality.

When Harding Lawrence heard of their decision he checked with other Braniff executives and then announced that he was putting the Braniff account in the hands of the new agency. He also offered advice in financing. Mary and her two partners each put up $30,000 and with a bank loan of $100,000 arranged through a business contact of Lawrence's, they were solvent.

They rented seven rooms in the Gotham Hotel on the corner of New York's Fifth Avenue and 55th Street and began operating as an advertising agency. The only "desks" they had in those first hectic weeks were card tables, and since there were no file cabinets business letters had to be "filed" in dresser drawers.

Telephones rang incessantly in the seven-room suite and for the first few days Mary and her partners could do nothing but answer questions from eager callers:

"Can I come to work for you? I'm ready to quit my job today and work for your new agency for less than my present salary if you'll just give me a chance!"

"Can you use some additional investment money? I can invest up to a million dollars. Your new agency is bound to be a success—I know a winning team when I see one!"

"Would you consider taking our ad account? We have a new product coming out next fall and need an agency with wit and sophistication to launch it. . . ."

The calls were coming in at such a frantic pace that Mary sent an SOS to her mother asking her to serve temporarily as a telephone girl. Violet Berg agreed delightedly. Through the years her help to her daughter had been psychological. Now, at last, she had a chance to work with her hands in helping the new agency get a start.

With the pressure of telephone calls relieved, the three partners were able to concentrate on organizing themselves into a stable firm. Mary Wells was named president; Richard Rich, treasurer and copy chief; Stewart Greene, secretary and art director of Wells, Rich, Greene, Incorporated. Office space was located. In May the new agency set up shop at 575 Madison Avenue—the street that has become a symbol for American advertising.

"Can WRG Make It?" a gossip columnist asked. "Can they get off the launch pad with just one account? Or will they have to go out and beat the bushes for business to keep their new agency going?"

To counteract this kind of sniping, Mary called in a news reporter and said frankly, "We don't solicit accounts—and never have. They come to us and we only take the ones we can't resist."

She then announced that the agency had signed contracts

to handle advertising for Personna Blades and Benson and Hedges' 100's.

"We're going to attract the cream of younger advertising talent in town," she said. "We want to make money, of course, and we want to upgrade our lives by two generations. But the whole point is that we want to produce the most wonderful and exciting advertising that's ever been done."

The first year meant incredibly hard work for Mary, her partners, and every one of the staff members they picked. Richard Rich said, "The campaigns have to be good. Later a momentum will build up—but now everybody's watching us."

The ad campaigns for Personna and especially for Benson and Hedges were so cleverly done and attracted so much favorable attention from the public that some of the giants of American business began to consider switching from established agencies to this new shop. A year after it was founded its clients included Hunt-Wesson Foods, General Mills, and American Motors. With annual billings of $70 million (which brought 15–20 percent commission to the agency) the new team won a place among the top thirty advertising agencies in the country.

The word went out along Madison Avenue that WRG was a shop to watch. They were making a reputation for ad campaigns that used humor and impertinence—a balloon man smoking a long cigarette and popping his own balloons —and their television commercials became famous as minimovies, compressed stories that left the TV viewer chuckling.

Wells, Rich, Greene continued to handle the advertising for their charter account—Braniff. In late autumn of 1966 Mary told close friends that she was engaged to marry Harding Lawrence. She flew to Paris with her daughters, Catherine and Pamela, in late November and was married at the Paris Town Hall to the airline executive.

To fulfill her dual role as a career woman and wife of a

prominent airline executive, Mary schedules her time carefully. She spends the early part of the workweek in New York and long weekends, usually beginning on Thursday, in Dallas with her husband and her daughters.

Reporters who had printed endless stories about Mary Wells, "The Wonder Woman of Advertising," continued to look to Mary Wells Lawrence for the unexpected—and controversial.

For American Motors—although she was bucking the advice of some top executives—she devised television commercials that showed men with sledgehammers battering a "Brand X" car to show how flimsy the construction was.

When Smith, Kline, and French drug-firm executives asked about buying up a floundering cosmetics company, she warned bluntly, "Don't buy it—you'll get stuck with its image. Originate your own—something daring."

Her approach in all of these campaigns was keyed to using the bold stroke, as she had with Braniff, to jolt the public into paying attention.

"If you want the public to notice you, you have to impress them," she told a meeting of young ad trainees. "You have to make waves—not ripples!"

You have to make waves. The words had the unquestionable ring of authority. Twenty years before, on her first ad-writing job in a Youngstown department store, the girl who was to become famous as an advertising trend setter studied an ad that said just "SALE" and resolved to find a different way, a daring way, to reach the public.

Today even her critics agree: She found it.

"A Shape Began to Emerge . . . ."

James D. Watson

He was a loose-limbed, rumpled young American with brittle hair that bushed around a boyish face. As he loped along the streets of Naples, Italy, that spring of 1951 he tried to keep warm and optimistic.

To twenty-two-year-old Jim Watson, visiting Naples had seemed like a fine idea at first. He would have a chance to get away from the chill of the University of Copenhagen and come south to "sunny Italy" for a scientific meeting during March and April.

But there was no heat in the zoological station where he attended lectures and no heat in the cramped room with its ancient furniture where he slept. Naples in spring was hardly the balmy paradise pictured in travel posters! He was numb with cold and beginning to feel frustrated.

The trip had been planned originally as part of Jim's last big push to master advanced chemistry. He could not dodge it any longer—as his professors in America were quick to remind him! He had breezed through the University of Chicago, graduating at nineteen. Then he had gone on to win a Ph.D. in biology at Indiana University. But in both colleges he had "sidestepped some of the tough courses in chemistry and physics," as he later admitted. Now, on the brink of doing really important research in microbiology, he was handicapped by the holes in his knowledge. He had to plug them.

The professors at Indiana University who had guided his Ph.D. studies and seen great promise in his brilliant mind had recommended Jim for a fellowship at the University of

Copenhagen. It would give him $3000 for a year's study. And in that year they hoped he would master chemistry— once and for all.

The year was fast drawing to an end. Jim had made some progress in spite of the fact that his professor at Copenhagen spoke only halting English. But he was not over the top by any means. He did not have the knowledge to go on in his study of genes. In midtwentieth century, this was where the scientific excitement was to be found.

Research on genes had captured the imagination of some of the most brilliant scientists in the world. Top researchers at the Rockefeller Institute and at the great universities— Columbia, Massachusetts Institute of Technology, California Institute of Technology—were working in teams to try to crack the secrets of heredity.

It was known that information inherited by an organism to make it what it is—whale or hummingbird, mongoose or man—was locked miraculously in the nucleus of the cell; specifically, in the nucleic acid. Nucleic acid—deoxyribose nucleic acid, or DNA for short—transmitted the "code of life."

But how did it function? What was the chemistry involved? How did it "pattern"? These were the big questions that top scientists were striving to answer in the 1950s.

As Jim Watson scuttled through the streets of Naples that chilly spring he started daydreaming. What if *he* were to crack the secret of the gene? What if *he* were to beat all the great biologists to the finish line in this race? James Dewey Watson, Jr. of Chicago would be world-famous. The Nobel Prize Committee would certainly recognize an achievement like that. And he would have his pick of positions at the great universities and research institutes.

It would be a real plum—especially if he could do it before he got too old. What was the good of being a great scientist if you were discovered when you were dead. . . .

The idea was wild and improbable, but it helped keep his

spirits up. Without dreams he would have been utterly depressed.

"I daydreamed about discovering the secret of the gene," he wrote later, "but not once did I have the faintest trace of a respectable idea."

The word "scientist" conjures up for many people the image of a stern-faced man in starched white lab coat, working from dawn until midnight in a sterile workshop. Science requires disciplined investigation, and the young person going into the field must be geared to work with tremendous concentration and perseverance.

Jim Watson had a full measure of discipline, certainly. But the stereotype ended there. He could work tirelessly on a project, but he believed in having as much fun along the way as possible. If he worked a fourteen-hour stretch on Monday he was likely to look for a tennis partner on Tuesday afternoon or—even better—a party on Tuesday night.

The bright young people at European colleges fascinated him. They did brilliant work in the laboratories but managed to find time to give wonderful parties where talk ranged from gossip about girls to discussions of the quantum theory. Being part of the new generation of scientists suited Jim perfectly. He had first-class brains (he had entered college at fifteen), an appealing smile, and an air of delicate health that prompted older scientists to help him with experiments—and their wives to invite him home for high-calorie dinners.

It was agreed that this young man from Chicago would make a solid contribution to science—someday.

At this point, though, he was stuck on dead center. James Dewey Watson, Jr. was born in Chicago in 1928. As a boy he pursued two hobbies that set the pattern for his later success. The first was studying birds. His father, who worked for a correspondence school, was an amateur ornithologist. On weekends he and Jim would prowl the parks around Chicago photographing swifts, nighthawks, and other species.

The second hobby, though, was strictly Jim's own: It consisted of soaking up facts, an amazing amount of them, and storing them in his memory as efficiently as a computer stores information. The *World Almanac* was a special favorite when he was about ten years old. His parents and his younger sister, Elizabeth, thought it a bit unusual but finally just accepted the fact that Jim *enjoyed* poring over books.

It did prove a profitable hobby after a while. Jim Watson could rattle off dates, figures, and facts so accurately that he won a regular assignment on a radio show, "The Quiz Kids," broadcast from coast to coast in the late 1930's.

At school Jim was known as one of the brightest—and shyest—students in his class. He had no special interest in science, though, until he read *Arrowsmith* by Sinclair Lewis. This novel about a dedicated young scientist triggered an ambition. Perhaps, like Martin Arrowsmith, *he* could make a scientific discovery someday that would benefit mankind too. . . .

His grades were so high that when he was fifteen—and after only two years of high school—he was accepted at the University of Chicago. The boyhood interest in birds led him to major in zoology, and he received a B.S. in 1947, when he was 19.

Although he made an excellent record at Chicago U.—known for its stiff courses—Jim had neatly sidestepped taking any chemistry or physics courses "which looked of even medium difficulty," as he later confessed.

When Indiana University accepted him for graduate work the professors there advised him, in no uncertain terms, to enroll immediately for organic chemistry. He had postponed it long enough. But they quickly changed their minds one afternoon when he tried heating benzene over a Bunsen burner!

Writing about his mistake in his story, *The Double Helix*, he says that his teachers judged it "better to turn out an uneducated Ph.D. than to risk another explosion."

Jim Watson was far from being "uneducated," though. To

earn his Ph.D. he did a thesis on the effects of radiation on the viruses that attack bacteria. His supervising professor, an Italian-born microbiologist named Salvador Luria, was delighted with this lanky young man from Chicago and encouraged him to get a fellowship for postdoctoral study at the University of Copenhagen in Denmark. He had to learn enough chemistry to understand the biochemical secrets of genes, Luria pointed out, and Copenhagen was the place to do it.

Armed with a grant from the National Research Council that gave him $3000 for one year of study, he sailed to Denmark in the autumn of 1950. Herman Kalckar, a biochemist who was highly regarded by Luria, was to be his teacher. Certainly *now* Jim Watson would master organic chemistry! Once he had a firm grasp of it he could go on to the toughest, most sophisticated problems in genetics.

Unfortunately, Kalckar's English was not fluent and Jim found that he was getting only the haziest concepts from him. He gravitated to the lab of another biologist and was just completing a project there when he learned about the conference in Naples.

But Naples also proved disappointing. Not only was it cold indoors as well as out, but most of the papers read by the scientists were unimportant. Then one afternoon Jim attended a lecture by someone named Maurice Hugh Frederick Wilkins of the University of London—and he immediately forgot how cold and bored he had been.

Wilkins explained in dry, precise terms that he had pulled a fiber out of a sticky gel of DNA and examined it with polarized light under the microscope. Next he had used a method called crystallography: He shot X rays through the fiber to see how individual atoms bent and scattered the X-ray beams. What he observed made him strongly suspect that DNA had a "crystalline structure." By way of illustration he flashed on the screen an X-ray diffraction picture of the structure.

The effect on Jim Watson was electrifying.

"Suddenly I was excited about chemistry," he said later. "Before Maurice's talk I had worried about the possibility that the gene might be fantastically irregular. Now, however, I knew that genes could crystallize; hence they must have a regular structure that could be solved in a straightforward fashion."

Would Wilkins accept him as a collaborator? After the lecture Jim started searching for him, but he had vanished.

The next day an excursion had been planned for the scientists to visit Greek temples outside Naples. Waiting for the bus, Jim spotted the elusive scientist. He introduced himself and began to talk excitedly about his interest in DNA. Wilkins, though, had too much English reserve to warm up to this brash young American. He made it clear that he wanted no part of such a scientific collaboration.

The conference in Naples came to an end a few days later. For Jim, it was back to Denmark and "the prospect of more biochemistry to avoid."

He put Wilkins's snub out of his mind. But he could not forget the DNA photograph. It seemed a "potential key to the secret of life. The fact that I was unable to interpret it did not bother me. It was certainly better to imagine myself becoming famous than maturing into a stifled academic who had never risked a thought."

If X-ray diffraction techniques could show the structure of DNA, then *this* might be a road to explore—but not at the University of Copenhagen. He had to switch to another lab. Working with Wilkins at the University of London would have been ideal, but . . . it was not to be. He would just have to look around for another arrangement.

Geneva was on the route back to Copenhagen and when Jim left Naples he stopped off for a visit with Jean Weigle, a Swiss biologist. Weigle, who was recently back from a winter of research at the California Institute of Technology, had heard a lecture by Linus Pauling, a member of the faculty of Cal Tech and the world's leading authority on the theory of chemical bonding. Pauling had advanced the theory that protein molecules were arranged in the twisting pattern of a helix; i.e., curved like the stripes in a pepper-mint stick.

With a real flare for showmanship, Pauling had unveiled a model of what he called the alpha helix and implied that, while it was still just theory, he might be on the road to solving the structure of DNA.

Again Jim Watson got excited. He knew and revered the work of Linus Pauling, who was considered one of the real geniuses of science and was sure to win a Nobel Prize for one of his discoveries. Working in his lab at Pasadena, California, 6000 miles away from Europe, he might very well have hit on the pattern that would apply to the nucleic acid as well as to proteins.

In the international race to solve DNA, Pauling could cross the finish line first.

It was evident, though, that Pauling was attacking the problem from a chemist's point of view. He was using X-ray diffraction techniques but none quite so advanced as those that thirty-five-year-old Maurice Wilkins had displayed in Naples. Wilkins and his woman associate at the University of London, Rosalind Franklin, were depending on X-ray techniques to give them the answer to DNA. Linus Pauling, on the other hand, was counting primarily on his genius in chemistry to do it.

To Jim Watson it seemed that *both* attacks might bring it off. If he could switch from the University of Copenhagen to a first-rank lab he might be able to build on both Pauling's and Wilkins's work to solve the riddle.

Going down the list of labs that might take a young American Ph.D. who frankly admitted that he was deficient in advanced chemistry and physics, he hit on Cambridge. A well-known Austrian-born biochemist named Max Perutz was working at the Cavendish Laboratory there and Professor Luria, Jim's old teacher at Indiana, knew Perutz well.

A letter to Indiana brought happy results: Luria wrote Perutz and recommended that the young biologist be given a place on one of the research teams at Cambridge. Perutz, in turn, smoothed the way with the director of the Cavendish Laboratory, Sir William Lawrence Bragg. In October, 1951, James Dewey Watson of Chicago, full of "youthful arrogance" as he put it and convinced that the secret of DNA was "up for grabs," arrived at Cambridge University.

Cutting his ties with Copenhagen meant that Jim had put his fellowship in jeopardy. He wrote a letter to the lab director saying that he wanted to give up conventional biochemistry because he believed it "incapable of telling us how genes work."

"Instead I told them that I now knew that X-ray crystallography was the key to genetics."

But the National Research Council had given him $3000 to study chemistry. Switching from the University of Copenhagen to another laboratory—even one as eminent as Cambridge—impressed them as being impulsive. The grant would *not* be renewed for the upcoming year, he was informed. The council had decided that he could not "benefit" from research at Cambridge. They implied that he was not quite ready to use multimillion-dollar lab equipment to solve the greatest genetic riddle of the twentieth century!

There was more than a grain of truth in this. Not only was Jim deficient in chemistry and math but also in physics. On his first day at Cambridge he had a conversation with scientist Max Perutz that was a mind-boggling experience.

"I did not follow Max at all," he confessed. "I was even ignorant of Bragg's Law, the most basic of all crystallographic ideas."

Bragg's Law, as most students of college physics know, is the basis of X-ray diffraction techniques. It had been worked out by a father-and-son team, Sir William Henry and Sir William Lawrence Bragg, who shared a Nobel Prize in 1915.

Sir William Henry Bragg had died in 1942. But in 1951, when young Jim Watson, bursting with ambition, came striding into Cambridge to work in the Cavendish Laboratory, Sir William Lawrence Bragg, co-discoverer of crystallography, was still very much alive. He was, in fact, *director* of the Cavendish Laboratory.

Sir Lawrence was a handsome, white-mustached figure with a formal manner. Sitting erectly behind his desk in the director's office at the Cavendish Laboratory, in his well-cut English suit, he looked every inch the eminent scientist. He may or may not have suspected the truth about the limited learning of the rumpled young American who had popped up. He welcomed him graciously, though. If Sir Lawrence had been Saint Peter welcoming Jim at the pearly gates, the young scientist could not have been happier. Cambridge, to him, was heaven.

One of the oldest universities in the world, with some of its colleges dating back to 1300, Cambridge has buildings of breathtaking beauty. As Jim began exploring the historic colleges that make up the Cambridge complex, his eyes scanned great medieval towers and spired chapels overlooking quadrangles and ancient greens.

"I had never seen such beautiful buildings in all my life," he wrote. "Any hesitation I might have had about leaving my life as a biologist vanished."

There was only one drawback: Cambridge was cold and damp. Even the Cavendish Laboratory had no central heating. But Jim had been cold in Copenhagen and Naples—and frustrated as well. Here in Cambridge he could put discomfort out of his mind. He had been assigned to a research team headed by a young scientist, John Kendrew. Their immediate goal was to study the protein myoglobin. There would be free time, though, and Jim was determined to learn crystallography and do his own probing of DNA.

The problem of finding a room—"digs" as the English call them—was solved when the Kendrews offered Jim a tiny room in their house on Tennis Court Road. He described it as "unbelievably damp and heated only by an aged electric heater." John and Elizabeth Kendrew kept the rent to a minimum, though, and this was more important than comfort. Jim had left Copenhagen with $1000 saved from his $3000 fellowship grant. He was not being paid to work at Cambridge, and if he was to make the $1000 last until he made a "great discovery" he would have to skimp on room and food.

Scientists at the Cavendish Laboratory ranged from the Nobel Prize-winning director, Sir Lawrence Bragg, and internationally known scientists like Max Perutz down to such unknowns as Jim Watson.

Another of the unknowns was Francis Harry Compton Crick, a thirty-five-year-old Englishman with a sharp nose and piercing eyes. Crick had a brilliant mind that could tackle the most profound problems in physics and math and apply them to biology. His own studies as a physicist had been interrupted by World War II and he had never been able to complete work for his Ph.D.

When Crick entered Cambridge in 1949 to do predoctoral work as a biophysicist, he was assigned to a team headed by Max Perutz. Perutz had been collecting X-ray diffraction data from hemoglobin crystals for eight years. Their immediate supervisor was Sir Lawrence Bragg, who, as a co-founder of crystallography, was fascinated by the X-ray possibilities in the Perutz experiment.

If Bragg was a theorist and Perutz an experimentalist, Francis Crick was a bit of both. Although he had only a portion of the formal schooling of some men at the Cavendish, he was so naturally brilliant that he theorized in daring, intuitive leaps.

"Often he came up with something novel—would become enormously excited, and immediately tell it to anyone who would listen," Watson writes. Unfortunately, Francis Crick's daring leaps of theory did not always prove sound. When this happened he had to go back to tedious—but essential—experiments.

The scientists at the Cavendish enjoyed Crick's "manic moments," Watson discovered. "They did a great deal to liven up the atmosphere of the lab, where experiments usually lasted several months or years." Crick talked almost as fast as he thought. His machine-gun delivery and boom-ing laugh could be frequently heard echoing through the halls of the Cavendish. There was one person, though, who was not particularly amused by Crick: Sir Lawrence Bragg. When the scientists stopped work to take morning tea and exchange ideas and gossip, Sir Lawrence usually sipped his in the director's office upstairs rather than risk "enduring Crick's booming over the tearoom," as Watson described it.

But even this retreat was not always safe. Twice Sir Lawrence had opened his office door to find water sloshing down the hall. Crick had incorrectly hooked up the tubing around a suction pump and, turning his back on it, had lost himself in a new theory!

But if Sir Lawrence was unnerved by Francis Crick, Jim Watson was not. Talking with the rapid-fire biophysicist was a joy. Crick was as excited about DNA as Jim was. Both had hunches about how genes were put together and be-grudged time spent on their formal assignments. They felt that if they could just put everything else aside and collabo-rate on DNA they might be able to crack it before Linus Pauling did!

In the two years that Crick had worked at the Cavendish he had concentrated resolutely on Perutz's hemoglobin re-search. But with Jim Watson in the lab, "always wanting to talk about genes," as he put it, "Francis no longer kept his thoughts about DNA in a back recess of his brain."

They talked over lunch at the Eagle pub and over dinner when Crick's French-born wife, Odile, invited Jim to eat at the Cricks' tiny flat. Even more important, they exchanged ideas at the Cavendish in their spare time.

Analyzing Pauling's recent success with the alpha-helix, they decided that "the same tricks might also work for DNA." Crick pointed out that Pauling's approach had been to rely on the basic laws of structural chemistry. He had asked himself which atoms "like to sit next to each other." Then he had constructed a three-dimensional model dupli-cating the atomic structure.

There are scientists who patiently plod toward a goal and

others who want to gallop. Crick was a galloper and so was Watson. Neither had made any real reputation in science, so if they failed with DNA they could chalk it up to experience.

If Pauling had taken a simple approach and scored so brilliantly, why shouldn't they? Their plan was simple: They would work with a three-dimensional model also, in the same way that a child clicks wheels and knobs together to build a toy windmill.

"They were brashly optimistic that the structure would say something about the basic unit of life," a scientist wrote later, "and it was either incredible luck or perhaps a stroke of genius that it did."

The advance of scientific knowledge in any field has been compared to a mountain-climbing expedition. A team of climbers sets a goal, reaches it, and establishes a "base camp." From this base camp another team goes out, climbing higher until they can establish their base camp at greater elevation. So it goes until the day a research team reaches the summit.

When James Watson and Francis Crick set out in 1951 to solve the mystery of DNA they began near the "summit" because of scientific "base camps" that had already been staked out by other dedicated scientists.

One such dated back to 1869. Frederick Miescher, a Swiss scientist, suspecting that the nuclei of cells held important clues to heredity, determined to find the biggest nucleus and do his research with it. It happened to be found in the pus cell. To obtain a supply he gave himself a grim chore: He washed bandages at a local hospital and was able to isolate a gummy gray powder from the pus-cell nucleus. When it was later found to be an acid it was named "nucleic acid" and, still later, "deoxyribose nucleic acid," or DNA for short.

Research was to show that DNA was thread-shaped and was, comparatively, a giant of a molecule. It weighed almost six million times as much as an atom of hydrogen! In spite of its size, however, it could not be seen even magnified

Arthur Ashe

Ralph Nader

Neil Simon

Mary Wells

James D. Watson

Edward Villella

Carl B. Stokes

Peggy Fleming

Bill Moyers

Shirley Verrett

300,000 times by the electron microscope. Scientists theorized that it was long but very, very thin.

In 1944 Prof. Oswald Avery of the Rockefeller Institute and two of his students definitely identified DNA as "the transmitting agent" in all heredity transactions. It was DNA that insured that the offspring of hummingbirds would be hummingbirds—and not sparrows or wrens—and the offspring of adult humans would be infant humans.

The "information" transmitted from one generation to another was locked in the nucleic acid of its genes—but how did this nucleic acid or DNA do its work? This was the big question that fascinated biochemists in the middle of the twentieth century.

In the spring of 1951, Linus Pauling announced the findings of his research at Cal Tech: Certain protein molecules called "polypeptide chains" were helical in shape—twisted like the stripes in a barber pole. It was not farfetched to assume, then, that the DNA structure would be a helix too.

William Astbury, a British scientist, had calculated in 1938—thirteen years before Pauling's "alpha helix"—that DNA would have a spiral-stairway look to it: There would be flat "plates" going off at right angles to the long axis of the molecule. And an American working at Columbia University, Dr. Erwin Chargaff, had predicted that the plates would be of four types: guanine, cytosine, adenine, and thymine.

Finally there was the work of Maurice Wilkins. Wilkins had been working at the University of London on the structure of DNA. His approach, and that of a woman collaborator, Rosalind Franklin, depended mainly on X-ray diffraction. He and Miss Franklin were beginning to use this technique with such astounding precision that they were even able to measure the distances between the various atoms that made up the DNA molecule.

If astronomers train telescopes on outer space to learn the secrets of our universe, microbiologists train their tools on inner space to learn its secrets. We can get some idea of the achievement of Wilkins and Franklin when we remember the size of an atom. Some three billion atoms can be contained in the ink of the period ending this sentence. Yet they were able to measure the distances between them!

It was Maurice Wilkins's report in Naples that first triggered Watson's excitement about DNA. Now that Watson was working on a research team at Cambridge it seemed logical that Wilkins would consider either collaborating or sharing his findings. When Jim mentioned the possibility to Francis Crick, though, Crick quickly vetoed it. It just wasn't done this way in England! Wilkins and "Rosy" Franklin were doing pioneering work on DNA in *their* laboratory in London, and other English scientists—even the most famous —were careful not to intrude.

Crick knew Wilkins well. The two men occasionally lunched together when Crick was in London. They did talk research over the lunch table, and Crick was kept up-to-date on some of Wilkins's findings. But an all-out collaboration just was not possible.

It was clear that if Watson and Crick were going to beat Pauling to the finish line they would have to rely on their own brainwork—and occasional *hints* from Wilkins's lab.

They began work with paper and pencil, trying to figure out roughly how the DNA structure would be patterned. Next they planned to construct a model. But they were fuzzy on the chemistry.

"Francis, as well as I, knew almost nothing about how inorganic ions were arranged in three dimensions," Watson says. "We had to face the bleak situation that the world authority on the structural chemistry of ions was Linus Pauling himself."

One day after lunch they dashed off to search for a copy of Pauling's classic book, *The Nature of the Chemical Bond.*

"A rapid reading was made of the relevant sections. This produced the correct values for the exact sizes of the candidate inorganic ions," Jim comments, "but nothing that could help push the problem over the top."

In November, 1951, Rosalind Franklin was scheduled to lecture in London and display new X-ray pictures of her DNA research. Watson had been at the Cavendish Laboratory for six weeks and had picked up enough basic knowledge about X-ray diffraction to follow it and pick up some clues.

He took the train to London on a "heavy, foggy night" and listened to the lecture. In a dry, completely unemotional tone, Miss Franklin reported on the progress of her work. It was proceeding slowly. She was not pessimistic about finding the structure of DNA—but she was not overly optimistic, either. With cautious reserve she pointed out that "further data" would have to be collected.

Watson returned to Cambridge on a late train and the next day excitedly gave a report to Crick. Jim had listened to the lecture with deep concentration—but had not taken any written notes. Crick was annoyed with his vague details. But they probably knew enough to start building a model.

"Perhaps a week of solid fiddling with the molecular models would be necessary to make us absolutely sure we had the right answer," Watson speculated. "Then it would be obvious to the world that Pauling was not the only one capable of true insight into how biological molecules were constructed."

On the basis of what Watson had seen and heard at Rosalind Franklin's lecture, they concocted a model with three sugar-phosphate legs to which the nucleotides were attached on the outside. Even though they used only some fifteen "atoms" in the structure, these kept falling out of the clamps set up to hold them. Both Watson and Crick found model building a frustrating business the first morning!

"After tea, however, a shape began to emerge which brought back our spirits," Watson writes. "Three chains twisted about each other in a way that gave rise to a crystallographic repeat every twenty-eight angstroms along the helical axis. This was a feature demanded by Maurice's and

Rosy's pictures, so Francis was visibly reassured as he stepped back from the lab bench and surveyed the afternoon's effort."

Crick was so elated that he hastily put through a call to London and invited Maurice Wilkins to Cambridge to examine the masterpiece. When Wilkins stepped off the train the next day he was accompanied by Rosalind Franklin and two men associates from the London laboratory. The model would have to pass inspection by all four!

The next two hours were an ordeal. The critics peered at the spiky copper-wire model from every angle and fired an incessant barrage of questions. Rosalind Franklin was especially blunt. It was evident to her that much of the structuring was based on data in her recent lecture. But the young American had simply not remembered it accurately!

Watson later summed up the confrontation this way:

"The awkward truth became apparent that the correct DNA model must contain at least ten times more water than was found in our model. This did not mean that we were necessarily wrong—with luck the extra water might be fudged into vacant regions on the periphery of our helix. On the other hand, there was no escaping the conclusion that our argument was soft."

By the time the four visitors from London went off to get their train, Watson and Crick were red-faced and thoroughly deflated. If DNA was to give up its secrets to them, they would have to find a structure based on arguments that were not "soft."

The invitation, issued so eagerly, backfired. When Wilkins and Franklin returned to their own laboratory at the University of London they complained to their chief that Francis Crick "and the American" were duplicating research on DNA. He, in turn, complained to Sir Lawrence Bragg, and Sir Lawrence called Crick and Watson on the carpet. He had checked their rickety copper model and was not convinced that it would revolutionize biochemistry. Further,

Max Perutz, who was Crick's immediate supervisor, and John Kendrew, Jim's supervisor, had been asked to give an opinion. Not original, they said.

"Abandon this DNA project," Sir Lawrence told them, "and get on with your formal research."

Both felt that it was useless to appeal his verdict. DNA was vastly more important than anything else being researched at the Cavendish Laboratory—they were still sure of that. And they were still determined to beat Linus Pauling. But the model they had produced based on sugar-phosphate cores was simply wrong.

"Any model placing the sugar-phosphate backbone in the center of a helix forced atoms closer together than the laws of chemistry allowed," Watson concluded. When they managed to put one atom "the right distance from its neighbor" they found that another "jammed impossibly close to its partners." It was maddening.

Francis Crick went doggedly back to work on his Ph.D. Jim tackled research on TMV, the tobacco mosaic virus. DNA rated only an occasional mention when they lunched together at the Eagle pub. The copper-wire model remained at the Cavendish lab for a few weeks and then was offered to Maurice Wilkins. In a halfhearted way, Wilkins replied that the next time someone from Cambridge happened to be in London, the jigs could be dropped off. Perhaps "someone might be found to put something together."

If there were disappointments and setbacks at the Cavendish Laboratory, there were compensations at Cambridge that spring of 1952 that made life distinctly bearable. Tennis and parties with pretty English girls—"popsies" they were called—livened the weekends. There were also invitations to house parties at English estates and visits to Oxford, England's other historic university.

Jim Watson believed in hard work. He had learned early in life that nothing in science is achieved without discipline. But after spending hours in the laboratory and other hours poring over research papers in his cramped, cold room at night, he was ready to relax.

He had mastered a useful technique. He could bear down on a scientific problem with complete concentration, turning it over and over in his mind while he was working at the lab, eating meals, walking around the beautiful quadrangles and greens of Cambridge. But when he was in a holiday mood, he usually put the problem out of his mind.

There were exceptions, though. Occasionally a flash of thought would be so insistent that it would intrude on a party. A popsie would find the young American telling a witty story one minute and then suddenly drifting off to ask another biochemist what he thought about protein subunits being helically stacked.

Jim could "program" his mind to compute a certain problem in biochemistry. It processed data on regular work hours—usually. But when a big solution was ready it ignored time schedules. Party or no party, the answer came clicking out!

This kind of creative insight helped him solve his research problem on TMV. While Crick was concentrating on work for his doctorate, Jim probed the viruses which cause mottle on tobacco leaves. He chose TMV, as he puts it, because "a vital component was nucleic acid, and so it was the perfect front to mask my continued interest in DNA."

A German scientist had theorized that TMV had a structure in the form of a helix. When Watson discussed it one day with Francis Crick, however, Crick was skeptical. "My morale automatically went down," Jim said. But he still could not rid himself of the notion that the structure had "cozy corners." These would accommodate the correct number and arrangement of molecules.

At an odd time and place, the answer came. He describes it this way: "On a bus to Oxford the notion came to me that each TMV particle should be thought of as a tiny crystal growing like other crystals through the possession of cozy corners. Most important, the simplest way to generate cozy corners was to have the subunits helically arranged. The idea was so simple that it had to be right. Every helical staircase I saw that weekend in Oxford made me more confident that other biological structures would also have helical symmetry."

One way to confirm his hunch was to photograph the tobacco virus with the X-ray camera. X-ray diffraction techniques—which had stumped him completely when he first came to Cambridge—had to be mastered. A new supertube—a powerful rotating anode X-ray tube—had just been installed at the Cavendish Laboratory and one of the men who used it offered to teach Watson how to set it up for photographing TMV. The trick in revealing a helix was "to tilt the oriented TMV sample at several angles to the X-ray beam."

Patiently collecting samples of the virus and photographing them occupied Watson for weeks during the spring and early summer of 1952. Then late one night in midsummer, he went back to shut down the X-ray tube and develop a photograph he had taken at a 25-degree angle.

"The moment I held the still-wet negative against the light box, I knew we had it. The telltale helical markings were unmistakable."

Finding that the structure of TMV was a helix gave James Watson new prestige at the Cavendish Laboratory. He had been regarded as a young man capable of brilliant insights—but with an unfortunate habit of going off on a wild-goose chase when he and Crick talked DNA. Now he had a solid achievement to his credit.

Crick was as elated as Jim over the new find, but both agreed that it was something of a detour. It would not take them along the road to DNA. They needed a fresh start— and new inspiration. Both were to come, unexpectedly, that fall.

The International Biochemical Congress was being held in Paris that August and Watson arranged to attend it. Some 2000 scientists converged on the Sorbonne to hear lectures on all aspects of biochemical research. One of the star attractions was a lecture by Linus Pauling. The world-famous chemist from Cal Tech had such a magnetic personality and his sense of the dramatic was so well developed that he was mobbed by admirers when the lecture ended. Watson, standing at the fringe of the crowd, longing to talk with him, could hardly see the fuzz on Pauling's high-domed head.

He did have a chance to meet him—briefly—a few days later. Watson had gone to Royaumont, France, to attend a special meeting on bacteriophage, and Pauling and his wife were invited to attend a special luncheon. Watson wangled an introduction to the great man and asked about research being done at Cal Tech. But somehow he could not swing the conversation around to DNA.

When Mrs. Pauling heard young Watson mention Cambridge she asked a favor. Her son Peter was coming to the Cavendish Laboratory to work for his Ph.D. His supervisor, in fact, was to be John Kendrew. Would Watson be good enough to welcome Peter Pauling and show him around Cambridge?

Jim assured Mrs. Pauling that he would be happy to do the favor—adding, mentally, that it would *certainly* be no hardship if Peter's sister came to visit. Rumors had reached Cambridge all the way from Pasadena that Linda Pauling was a blond beauty who would "undoubtedly liven up the Cambridge scene."

Peter Pauling started his doctoral studies at the Cavendish Laboratory that fall and was assigned a desk in the office shared by Crick and Watson. It proved a practical arrangement. The excitement they had shared over DNA in the first months that Watson was at Cambridge had been defused by the failure of the model. They still talked theories once in awhile at lunch or strolling back to the laboratory. And sometimes the talks generated enough enthusiasm so that they "fiddled with the models" for a brief time when they got back. But when they reached a dead end Crick would drift away to his Ph.D. research, leaving Watson to carry on alone.

"Without Francis' reassuring chatter my inability to think in three dimensions became all too apparent," he admits.

Young Peter Pauling was good for morale at times like these. Cambridge had charmed him too, and when scientific problems became "pointless" he switched the conversation to parties and popsies.

One day a letter to Peter from his father mentioned that he had a "structure for DNA." The news electrified Crick and Watson. They asked to see the letter and read and re-read it feverishly, searching for details. But the chemist had given none.

Pacing up and down the office, Crick began spouting theories. He reviewed all the logical steps that Pauling must have taken, all the clues available to him. They were, after all, known to scientists throughout the Western world through scientific publications. What had the great chemist done in his laboratory at Cal Tech to make it all hang together? What were the unknown data he had discovered?

If Francis Crick could, with one brilliant insight, come up with the same data, he and Jim Watson could publish their findings and get equal credit.

Pacing the floor and brainstorming did not produce results, however, that day or the next or the next. Although neither Crick nor Watson mentioned to Sir Lawrence Bragg that they were again "thinking DNA" John Kendrew learned of it and was sympathetic. He even tried cheering them up. He reminded them that the most advanced X-ray pictures in the world were being taken by Wilkins and Franklin at the University of London. Linus Pauling was probing the problem 6000 miles away in California and it was not very likely that he could close in on DNA without intimate knowledge of the London data. But Crick and Watson were still fearful. All their work would be futile if Pauling had cracked the secret.

A month passed and Peter received a letter from his

father saying he had written a manuscript on DNA and would be sending a copy from Pasadena shortly. But again there was no hint of his approach. Again the collaborators became tense. Then one day in February, 1953, Peter walked into the office with his father's manuscript in his coat pocket.

"Seeing that neither Francis nor I could bear any further suspense, he quickly told us that the model was a three-chain helix with a sugar-phosphate backbone in the center," Watson comments.

It sounded so close to the structure they had built in the copper-wire model that Watson impulsively pulled the manuscript out of Peter's pocket and raced through it to see exactly how Linus Pauling had positioned the essential atoms.

He scanned the summary and introduction and then studied the illustrations. Something was out of kilter in the man's figuring. Linus Pauling, known the world over for his genius in chemistry, had miscalculated!

"I realized that the phosphate groups in Linus' model were not ionized, but that each group contained a bonded hydrogen atom and so had no net charge. Pauling's nucleic acid in a sense was not an acid at all." He passed the manuscript to Crick, who confirmed the error. "I began to breathe slower," Watson says. "By then I knew we were still in the game."

The manuscript with its unorthodox chemistry was scheduled to be published in six weeks. Once the journal was in the hands of biologists and chemists they would take delight in pointing out to the great man his error in elementary chemistry! And Pauling would then work day and night to find the answer and redeem his reputation.

James Watson and Francis Crick were still in the game, but time was running out. To beat Pauling they would have to stop being part-timers and return to DNA full time.

As soon as he could arrange it, Watson went up to London to show the Pauling manuscript to Wilkins and Franklin. He talked first with Rosalind Franklin in her laboratory.

When he mentioned DNA and a probable helix structure she retorted hotly that her X-ray data indicated that there were *no* helices in DNA. She also insisted that in any three-dimensional model the sugar phosphate must be placed outside the nucleotides.

Later, in a lab down the hall, Wilkins brought out an X-ray print of a new form he called the "B" structure. "The instant I saw the picture my mouth fell open and my pulse began to race," Watson says. "The pattern was unbelievably simpler than those obtained previously ("A" form). Moreover, the black cross of reflections which dominated the picture could arise only from a helical structure."

Maurice Wilkins impressed on Watson that if Rosalind Franklin was wrong about the helix—and this "B" picture seemed to prove it—she was probably right, though, when she insisted that the bases should be in the center and the backbone outside.

Back at Cambridge the next morning, a Saturday when Crick was sleeping late, Watson confronted Sir Lawrence Bragg with the new evidence. He drew a rough sketch based on the "B" X-ray picture and showing DNA as a helix which repeated its pattern every thirty-four angstroms along the axis.

He gave a detailed report on Linus Pauling's error and stressed that he and Crick had a very good chance of cracking the secret—and bringing fame to the Cavendish Laboratory—if they could put other assignments aside and concentrate on it full time.

The arguments impressed Bragg and he finally agreed. Watson was elated. "I dashed down the stairs to the machine shop to warn them that I was about to draw up plans for models wanted within a week."

Reconstructing the DNA molecule to square with Rosalind Franklin's theory of the "backbone on the outside" raised new problems in the hectic days that followed. They had to rearrange the four nucleotides in such a way that the chemical bonding would hold them together.

Hour after hour they worked with pieces of wire and

metal from the Cavendish machine shop. Each tiny metal spoke or bracket was a stand-in for a part of the DNA molecule: the phosphate, the sugar, or one of the bases. In fitting the delicate pieces together, they found that all too often the atoms they had assigned to certain spots just should not be there. Either they were too close together or they would not bond. There could be only one right structure. It had to conform to immutable laws of chemistry. And it had to conform to the helix in the X-ray picture that Maurice Wilkins had just developed.

It got to be a maddening business that drove both young scientists to the limit of their patience. Was there *any* hydrogen-bonding scheme that squared with the X-ray evidence?

When a model was rigged incorrectly they had to dismantle it and start all over again. One pattern kept emerging, though: The sugar molecules and phosphates formed long, twisting lines. Attached to them at right angles were the four bases: adenine, guanine, cytosine, and thymine. The twisting lines formed a spiral ladder, with the sugars and phosphates making up the ladder "frames" and the bases making up the "rungs."

Both Watson and Crick were stumped, though, by the fact that the bases were of different sizes. Cytosine and thymine were smaller than adenine and guanine. The twisting ladder of DNA could hardly have "rungs" of different sizes!

Checking with the machine shop one afternoon, Watson was told that certain parts he had ordered would not be ready for two days. Exasperated, he went upstairs to his office and began cutting out chemical "bases" from stiff cardboard. It was almost dark when he finished. Since he was going to the theater that night with a group of Cambridge students and their dates, he left the pieces stacked on his desk and hurried across the campus to get ready.

Early the next morning when the lab was quiet, he set to work alone. In what was probably the most important jigsaw puzzle ever assembled, Watson began to piece together the cardboard bases. Methodically, systematically, he checked out all the conceivable hydrogen-binding possibilities.

After shifting the bases in and out of pairing patterns countless times, he began to sniff victory.

"Suddenly I became aware that an adenine-thymine pair held together by two hydrogen bonds was identical in shape to a guanine-cytosine pair held together by at least two hydrogen bonds."

Two bases—a long and a short—were required for each rung of the twisted helix ladder. And the only combinations that were valid were adenine paired with thymine, and guanine with cytosine. Clicked together, they could be fitted neatly in pairs between the sugar phosphates.

If it checked out, this could be the secret structure of DNA!

The only other person in the office that morning was Jerry Donohue, an American crystallographer with a formidable knowledge of chemistry. Watson called him over to his desk and asked if he "had any objection" to the new base pairs. With a practiced eye, Donohue scanned the cardboard pattern. It *could* work, he told Watson. This pairing was completely feasible.

A short time later Crick strolled down the corridor and appeared in the office doorway. Greeting him with a whoop, Watson blurted that "the answer to everything" was in their hands. Crick managed to maintain a cool skepticism for the first few minutes as he stood at the desk peering over the pattern. With nervous fingers he pushed the cardboard bases out of Watson's pattern and into another. Not plausible. He tried another. Not plausible. Another and still another. The only pattern that would satisfy the two criteria—hydrogen-bonding and the helix structure—was the one Watson had hit on: adenine with thymine and guanine with cytosine.

As Crick feverishly worked, checking for possible mistakes, he made a stunning discovery: The two bonds joining base and sugar of each pair were related by an axis at right angles to the twisting helix axis.

Watson saw the importance of his partner's discovery at once.

"Both pairs could be flipflopped over and still have their glycosidic bonds facing in the same direction," he wrote later. "It strongly suggested that the backbones of the two chains must run in opposite directions."

James Watson and Francis Crick were delirious with joy. They were lowly beginners in science compared with the eminent researchers who were trying to crack the secret structure of DNA, yet the victory was theirs.

A day or so later when the machine shop finally came through with the long-awaited parts, they constructed a three-dimensional model showing all the components that go to make up DNA. Each bristling wire spoke, thrusting out from a metal rod, was positioned at a precise distance from its neighbor. Then it was soldered securely in place so that it would not sag—or clatter to the floor.

One doubt still bothered Watson and Crick, though. Were the contacts "reasonable"? Did they satisfy the laws of chemistry? Building a model like this meant that it would have been "all too easy to fudge a successful series of atomic contacts so that, while each looked almost acceptable, the whole collection was energetically impossible," as Watson put it.

Crick—who once had loved sleeping late—now raced to the laboratory every morning to check and double-check these interatomic contacts. With a plumb line and measuring stick, he went over every inch of the model, writing down the atomic coordinates. They had claimed too much too soon for the first model. This one had to be perfect.

During these days of final testing, the model became a star attraction at the Cavendish Laboratory. Staff members, from graduate students to senior scientists, came and brought their friends to inspect the five-foot-high model, a curious right-handed helix with two twisting chains running in opposite directions. Here, in bristling wire and metal, the awesome building block that governs heredity had finally been given shape.

Sir Lawrence Bragg, who had been home with flu when the first cardboard pattern was made, returned to his office to see the metal model being tested. He congratulated Watson and Crick warmly but reminded them to be sure to recheck the organic chemistry with a Cambridge professor!

When Peter Pauling wrote his father describing the structure, Linus Pauling promptly accepted it as *the* answer. Maurice Wilkins came down from London to see it and left, determined to produce X-ray pictures that would confirm or be really definitive. Two days later he called Cambridge to say that he and Rosalind Franklin had X-ray data that strongly supported the double-helix theory.

"Rosy's instant acceptance of our model at first amazed me," says Watson. ". . . like almost everyone else, she saw the appeal of the base pairs and accepted the fact that the structure was too pretty not to be true."

Wilkins and his associates collaborated in writing up their findings and submitted a report to the British scientific journal *Nature* for April, 1953.

In the same issue was an article under the names of James Dewey Watson and Francis Crick. It began, "We wish to suggest a structure for the salt of deoxyribose nucleic acid (DNA). This structure has novel features which are of considerable biological interest." The report, written in simple, direct language, took only some 900 words and occupied a single page.

When it was read by biologists and chemists around the world the implications were clear: The young American from Chicago and the Englishman who had not yet completed work for his Ph.D. had made the single most important biological discovery of the twentieth century. The brilliant success that a gangling young biologist had longed for, one damp spring in Naples, had been achieved—as he had hoped—while he was still young.

James Dewey Watson had to wait nine years, however, to win the Nobel Prize. In 1962, when he was thirty-four and a professor at Harvard, he was summoned to Sweden. There he joined Francis Crick and Maurice Wilkins, whose X-ray work made their discovery possible. The three received the Prize for Medicine and Physiology and shared the $50,000 prize money.

A scientist who later worked on the synthesis of DNA, the "creation of life in a test tube," has summed up the Watson-Crick research this way:

"In spite of methods that were irregular, they established DNA as the material in the genes of living matter that accounts for heredity. Their structure with its 'novel features' laid the foundation for research in improving human life and even curbing cancer through genetic manipulation."

In the years since his history-making experiments with Francis Crick at Cambridge, Watson has spent his time in research and teaching. When supervising research projects of his graduate students he often persuades them to take a wild chance, to tackle scientific problems that look impossible to solve rather than plod along with one that will make a solid reputation—and not involve risk.

James Watson believes in taking risks, in following a scientific hunch even if it looks like a wild-goose chase—even if it involves losing a fellowship grant.

"I believe in the now," he says, "not in being discovered when you're dead."

"When Eddie Dances, Manliness Comes Into Ballet"

Edward Villella

It was Christmas night, 1955, and eighteen-year-old Edward Villella, a second-year cadet at the New York Maritime College, was on his way to his parents' house in Queens, New York. It was late and the streets were deserted, but he walked along with easy confidence. He had grown up in this neighborhood, and many of the houses with Christmas lights gleaming were the homes of friends whom he had once gone to school with at P.S. 130.

Suddenly from the dark a figure rushed at him, striking him a brutal blow on the head. Hours later when he was discovered and rushed to the hospital by his parents the doctors found that the blow from the mugger had caused a massive brain concussion. Both his eyesight and speech had been affected temporarily.

Full recovery would take months. After the stay in the hospital he would have a long convalescence at home.

"It's going to be a slow business," the doctors told Eddie and his parents, "but we'll get you back to Maritime."

We'll get you back to Maritime.

The doctors' words slipped in and out of his mind as he lay in the hospital bed. As soon as he was well enough he would go back to classes, and in two years he would graduate with a bachelor's degree in maritime transportation and start a career that would pay a handsome salary and offer a solid, secure future.

It was the kind of future that his mother and father wanted for him. Joseph Villella, who worked hard in his small trucking business, had reminded Eddie often that it was important for a boy to get a good education and train for a job that would give him security.

Maritime College, located at Fort Schuyler near the Bronx end of the Throg's Neck Bridge, is part of the university system of New York State and offers an excellent education at state expense. Since young Eddie had been a good student at high school, graduating when he was sixteen, the family encouraged him to apply. When he was accepted his parents were jubilant. The day he put on his cadet's uniform symbolized for them his first step toward an honorable and secure future.

The mugger's attack on Christmas night would put him behind in his studies. But Eddie Villella was both welterweight boxing champion and a member of the baseball team at Maritime and had made a host of good friends. His buddies would help him catch up on assignments.

If all went well, he would graduate with his classmates in two years and take his first assignment as a transportation officer in the merchant fleet. He was a lucky fellow: He had a nice secure future all sewed up.

Only one thing spoiled it—a life at sea was not what he wanted. He wanted to dance with a ballet company. Earlier he had studied dancing for five years and he knew that it was one of the world's riskiest, most unstable ways to earn a living. Some people even sneered that it was a sissy thing for a boy to do. But it didn't matter. Eddie Villella wanted with all his heart to dance with a ballet company.

By a strange coincidence, it was another blow on the head eight years before that had been his reason to try dancing. Ten-year-old Eddie loved to play ball—especially "running bases" with the other boys on his block. One afternoon as he was running for base, a friend pegged the ball too hard and not too accurately. It hit him squarely on the head.

Even now, years later, he remembers it vividly.

"I can still feel it," he says, putting the tips of his fingers gingerly at the base of his skull. "It came—*thock!*—right into the back of my head. I went out!"

This was a painful blow but not serious. His parents decided, though, that the doctor's advice to "keep Eddie quiet for awhile" should be strictly observed. He was not to play running bases or any other kind of ball for a month or two.

Keeping quiet was torture for this boy who had superabundant energy. But Mildred Villella was a woman of firm conviction. She kept him under close observation every afternoon—and, on days when his sister, Caroline, went to a dance studio in the neighborhood for her ballet lesson, young Ed went along. To a ten-year-old baseball hopeful, sidelined with an injury, the idea of spending afternoons at a dance studio watching little girls go through their ballet routines was grim.

The school Caroline attended was a small one in the neighborhood, but to Mrs. Villella it seemed a good place for her daughter to learn the basics. If she did well she could switch to a first-rate school, perhaps one of the famous ballet schools in Manhattan.

Ballet dancing, as Ed discovered the day of his first visit, attracts girls by the dozens—and boys not at all. Everywhere he looked he saw girls: The little dance studio was alive with them, bustling in and out, chattering to the receptionist. As they swirled around him he realized he was the only male on the premises. How dumb it was to be here instead of playing ball with the fellows that afternoon!

His sister popped into a dressing room and minutes later came out dressed in a leotard. As Ed watched from a rickety folding chair she took her place with the other students in the little studio and the lesson began. The studio was bare and almost barnlike. A scarred piano and some wooden chairs were the only furnishings, but the young students were too busy to mind. Caroline, like her classmates, lined up at a railing called a *barre* which had been built around three sides of the room. Eddie had heard his sister speak of "working out at the *barre*" and now he understood what that term meant. He saw girl after girl in leotard and soft practice shoes line up at this railing and go through a strange ritual. Holding the *barre* lightly with the left hand and standing erect, they placed their heels together and turned their feet outward as far as they could go. It was the first of the five basic positions they would master.

From the strange toes-out stance that looked almost like the start of a duck-walk, the girls slid the right foot to the side, balancing evenly on both feet, then scissored the legs into three different positions until the feet finally clicked to rest.

As the pianist played a tune with measured beat the students went through these five positions, and the woman teacher, in tights and filmy overskirt, walked up and down the line observing each girl closely to see that the feet were positioned correctly and smoothly, without jerkiness.

When she was satisfied that they had worked well with the right foot, she called out, "*Changé*, everyone!" and the girls reversed positions: They held the *barre* with the right hand and did their five positions with the left foot working.

Again and again the students went through the five positions while the pianist played a melody with a strong beat. When the teacher was satisfied that feet were being scissored correctly she set the girls to doing something she called "pliés" (plee-AY). Facing the *barre* and holding onto it, the girls stood with their feet flat on the floor and turned outward, as before, and then very slowly began knee bends.

"Watch turnout," the teacher called to the girls, and several students positioned their feet at a better angle.

"Back erect!" the teacher called and the girls straightened slack shoulders.

When the lesson was almost over, she called "Center practice!" and the students moved away from the walls and formed three rows facing a huge mirror. Again they went through the given positions and the pliés. This time, though, they worked without the steadying influence of the *barre*, and wobbles and jerkiness began to show up.

The teacher went from student to student pointing out errors: feet that had been forced too harshly into a turnout so that the ankles rolled forward; a back too arched or too slack. Even the students' arms and hands came under her scrutiny. Arms that jutted out at the elbow were taught to move close to the body, ". . . and softly," the teacher said. "Arms should move softly, easily."

At last the lesson was over, the students broke ranks and headed for the dressing room as the teacher reminded them they were due back again on Thursday at four—"promptly, please."

Twice-a-week visits to the dance studio with Caroline became a regular routine for Ed. "The first three or four times, I just watched," he recalls. "Then one day my mother suggested that I might as well take a lesson—it was better than killing time. So I did."

Surprisingly he found the sensation of being out on the smooth floor, moving to music, was not grim at all. It was fun. It was understood by all the family, though, that if Eddie took dance lessons at the little studio they were to be just a casual thing. Caroline was the serious dance student. She was going to be a ballerina some day.

When September came, Mrs. Villella found the school she wanted Caroline to enroll in: the famous School of American Ballet, which trained dancers for the New York City Ballet—its parent group—and for other professional dancing assignments from classical to Broadway musicals, movies, and TV.

The director of the school was George Balanchine, one of the most famous dance masters and choreographers in the world. As a young boy in Russia, Balanchine had been enrolled by his father in the Imperial Ballet School at Saint Petersburg. When the Russian czar, Nicholas II, was assassinated and the Communists took over the Russian government, Balanchine's school changed from "Imperial" to "State," but the dance courses remained as strict as ever. A child who was accepted for free ballet training by the Russian government had to undergo discipline as strict as in the army. The teachers enforced rigid rules for sleeping, eating, classroom lessons, and dance practice. The body had to be trained until it reached the peak of form: Girls could pirouette and boys leap with effortless ease to the music of great composers.

It was this kind of disciplined training that George Balanchine had received as a young man in Russia. The school he directed in New York was much less harsh and rigid, but there was a firm and unshakable insistence on discipline. When a Susie Jones stepped off the subway at Broadway and Eighty-second Street in New York and walked with her mother through the doors of Balanchine's school to take classes, she left her typical American self behind and became a humble apprentice, willing to sacrifice hobbies, sports, television, and even French fries and Cokes on the chance that years thence she might become a professional dancer.

Most mothers who hoped to enroll their daughters in the Balanchine school knew little of this background, however. They had heard simply that it was "tops." The only students accepted were those who auditioned for the teachers and showed promise.

Caroline auditioned early in September and to her mother's delight was accepted. Offhandedly Mrs. Villella mentioned that she had a son, a year younger than Caroline, who also danced.

"Bring him in," the teacher suggested. "Let's see what he can do."

One afternoon a few days later Eddie, Caroline, and their mother took the subway into Manhattan. From the exit on upper Broadway they walked to a building near Eighty-second Street and climbed a steep flight of stairs to the second floor.

The entrance hall was alive with young people. Here again, most of them were girls. When Eddie had changed to practice clothes he was shown to a studio where a woman asked him to dance for her.

As the pianist played a familiar tune, he went through the basic steps he had learned at the little studio in his neighborhood. The lady said nothing for a while but seemed to be watching very intently. After a while, she called in another teacher and then another. When the pianist finally stopped playing and the audition was over, she told Mrs. Villella that her son danced very well: The school would like to offer him a scholarship.

The woman who first recognized the potential of ten-year-old Eddie Villella was Muriel Stuart. She had once been a soloist with world-famous Anna Pavlova and also ballet mistress of the Chicago Civic Opera. Like many other dancers who go on to become dance teachers, she had a sure instinct for spotting talent and it seemed to her that the little dark-haired boy from Queens with well-proportioned legs and arms and an easy grace of movement might make a fine dancer.

In the months that followed, Eddie and Caroline settled into a routine that is standard for classical dance students all over America—and Europe: They mastered the steps based on the five basic positions, going over and over them for absolute precision.

The routine was far from toe dancing or a "prince and princess" whirling across the stage under colored lights to the music of Tchaikowsky. The nine- and ten-year-olds first had to concentrate on the "turnout" of the feet and legs before working up, gradually, to toe dancing.

Before a girl puts on blocked ballet shoes and begins to dance on her toes she has to study two years or more so that she has good control not only of her feet and legs but of her whole body—head, torso, arms. Ballet dancing is special: It is based not on natural movements of the body as modern dance is but on stylized movements that put terrific demands on the body. The spectacular leaps and jumps of the male ballet dancer and the graceful pirouettes of the ballerina dancing on her toes (on *pointe* as it is called) are learned little by little so that muscles are not strained or legs contorted into knots.

Many little girls whose teachers—or mothers—hurried them into dancing on their toes when they were too young and their bones too soft have grown up to be not graceful ballerinas but dance dropouts with foot problems.

Like other good dance schools around the country, the School of American Ballet insisted that students concentrate on the basics for two or three years before promotion to toe dancing for the girls and "men's classes" (leaps, jumps, and air turns) for boy students.

Eddie caught glimpses of long-legged sixteen- and seventeen-year-olds doing spectacular leaps in the men's classes and heard the older students talk about their chances of getting jobs in dance companies and on television. But it was a world he could only dimly imagine. It was as far beyond ten-year-olds doing bends at the *barre* as playing for the New York Yankees was beyond "running bases" in Queens.

Although baseball and ballet were worlds apart, Eddie was beginning to see that they did have some things in common. Training was important in both; you had to watch what you ate—stuffing on hamburgers and malts was fatal. You had to get plenty of sleep. And you had to exercise—stick to a regular routine, not be just hit-and-miss about it.

Ballet was really tougher, though, than a sport. It took hours and hours of practice—going through the routines so that the muscles began to respond automatically. That was it: You taught your muscles the pattern you wanted them to follow and they followed it. After a while you didn't have to *think* about a move you were going to make. It was automatic. But that was because you put a great deal of practice into it—practice and sweat.

It amazed Eddie to see the way dancers came out of the intermediate and advanced classes with their clothes wet with sweat. Shirts were not just patchy-damp. They were soaked. The young dancers did not seem to mind it, though. They came out of a studio laughing and joking and all charged up. They acted like baseball players who have just won a tough game.

For five years both Caroline and Eddie studied at the School of American Ballet. First it was two lessons a week, then three, and finally five. Fortunately, the scholarship that had been granted to Eddie was renewed continuously so that his parents paid only for Caroline's lessons. To Mrs. Villella it seemed a worthwhile investment: She still hoped with all her heart that her daughter would have a dancing career someday. But Caroline was growing restless. Dancing had demanded all her time, all her energy for too long. Finally, when she was sixteen she announced that she was giving it up.

The decision jarred her mother badly. Mildred Villella decided that if her daughter was giving up dancing, her son should pull out too.

Eddie was stunned. Dancing had become the most important thing in his life. "To live is to dance, to dance is to live," says Snoopy in the "Peanuts" cartoonstrip. In the five years Eddie took lessons at the School of American Ballet he had come to know exactly what that meant. When he was in the studio dancing he was living—at maximum intensity. The slow, careful limbering of muscles week by week and year by year had toned his body so perfectly that he was beginning to leap, twist, twirl with explosive power.

Ed, who was then 15, had been studying at New York's High School of Performing Arts. Dance instruction there as part of his regular school day, plus the lessons he was taking at the studio, was giving him the technique he needed to reach his goal: dancing with a great company like the New York City Ballet in tours all over the United States and in Europe.

He begged his parents to let him continue, but they would not change their minds. So long as Caroline was cutting her ties to dancing they wanted him to do it too. A great many teen-age boys would have reacted to such a decision by behaving spitefully or rebelliously toward their parents. Ed's reaction was grim—but obedient—acceptance.

He withdrew not only from the School of American Ballet ("I never told them why—I just stopped going to lessons") but also from the High School of Performing Arts. To prepare for college, he switched to a private high school in Manhattan and completed three years' work in two.

Redirecting his life and his future into new channels was a grim business, but he went through with it. "I loved my parents," he says simply. "They wanted me to do it."

The New York Maritime College, located just across the Throg's Neck Bridge from the Villella home, seemed a good choice, and at his parents' urging Eddie applied and was accepted. His friends told him how lucky he was to be going there as a cadet, but he recalls feeling anything but lucky. "Walking through the main gate that first day with my bags in my hands, I had a scared feeling. I was starting college—but I was missing out on what I *really* wanted to do in life."

Although his heart wasn't in it at first, he soon grew used to the cadet routine. On weekdays, reveille was at 6:15 A.M. and each cadet was expected to have his half of the two-man room ready for inspection before 6:50. Breakfast was at 7 and morning class periods lasted from 8 until 11:45. After lunch cadets attended class from 12:45 until 3:55. From then until the dinner call at 6:15 they were free to participate in either intramural or intercollegiate sports.

Sports became an important part of Eddie's life. When he felt restless and chafed at routine, the best remedy, he found, was to keep moving, keep active. He would grab a football and get his friends out to snap the ball around. Or he would go over to the gym, put on boxing gloves, and clout the punching bag.

He took the campus welterweight boxing championship

and won his letter in baseball. By the beginning of his second year, he was beginning to enjoy some—if not all—aspects of life at Maritime. Good looks, friendliness, and a quick smile made him popular. He describes his fellow cadets there as a "great bunch of fellows. We had real camaraderie."

Then on that fateful Christmas night in 1955, as he walked through deserted streets on his way to his parents' home, he was hit on the head by a mugger and suffered a massive brain concussion.

In the long weeks of convalescence that followed, Eddie Villella had time to analyze his life and his ambitions.

"We'll get you back to Maritime," the doctors had promised. But he did not want to go back. He wanted—with all his heart—to dance. The urge was too strong to be suppressed even for the parents he loved.

It was then that he made a secret promise to himself: As soon as he was well enough to be up and about he would go back to the studio.

One afternoon, three months later, he took the subway into Manhattan and headed down Broadway toward the School of American Ballet.

He climbed the steep flight of stairs and pushed open the door. The halls were empty. In one of the studios a pianist was playing a waltz with measured beat for the beginners. The first person he saw in the office was Natalie Molostwoff —"Miss Molo" to the children. As he walked to her desk, she glanced up and the look she gave him took in his Maritime uniform and the expression in his eyes.

Before she could say a word, he blurted out his question: "Is there a class I can take?"

"Studio B—they're just starting," she answered immediately. "Hurry!" No questions or comments. Not even "Hello." Eddie Villella was back. Conversation could wait for another time.

In the men's dressing room, he changed from his uniform to practice clothes and raced down the hall to Room B. As he walked to the *barre*, George Balanchine turned and saw him. "Well, look who's here!"

Again, no questions. Eddie was back and working out. It was almost as if he had never gone away.

For the next hour and a half he went through all the exercises, throwing himself into them with desperate energy—working all out. It was a crazy thing to do. He had not danced for a long time; his muscles were slack and he had gone through a long convalescence after the brain concussion. Tomorrow would be torture. Tomorrow he wouldn't even be able to walk! But it would be worth it.

The day that Eddie went back to the dance school something inside switched on. It was almost as if the last wire in an electrical circuit had been connected and current could go through. Giving his energies to anything other than dancing—even the merchant marine—would be dishonest.

He knew he would have to go back to Maritime for a while. He could not quit until he had prepared his parents. But the day would come. . . . He now had a goal to work toward. The nagging restlessness was over. He was going to be a dancer—one of the best, he hoped.

The next year was one of the most difficult of Eddie's life. As a cadet living and studying at the academy he had to "shape up" to its high standards. He had classes from early morning until late afternoon and after dinner there was little time to relax. Like all cadets he had to "hit the books." By scheduling his time down to the last minute he did manage to get in to dance classes, though.

How rusty he was! He had been away from dancing for almost four years. True, he was only nineteen. But watching the effortless leaps of the sixteen- and seventeen-year-olds in the adagio class, he felt ancient.

Dancers, even world-famous stars, must work out daily to keep agile. The routine is standard whether they are appearing in Tokyo or Topeka. Starting at the *barre*, they go through the basics—knee bends based on the five positions

—and then work up gradually to the most difficult steps and sequences.

For Eddie, away from the daily routine for years, the workouts meant torturous retraining of leg muscles, arm muscles, the whole body. His practice clothes were drenched with sweat and his body ached after each workout. But he was beginning to see results. In adagio, for instance, where the advanced students from both men's and girls' classes work together, he was lifting his partner smoothly now. The strength that had won him the welterweight championship at the academy was being harnessed in a different way: lifting a ballerina as if she were featherlight instead of 100 pounds of bone and muscle, carrying her halfway across the stage, and then tilting her at the correct angle so that she could dance away on *pointe*.

Besides his work of "partnering" the ballerinas, he was practicing the solo dance steps that are taught in men's classes. These must be mastered by advanced men students just as toe dancing (pointework) is mastered by the advanced girls. Showy and spectacular, these steps look difficult—and are. They include jumping over your own leg, clicking heels to right or left in midair, the Russian "cobbler" squat while shooting out each leg in turn, and the show-stopping leap and split in midair with hands shooting out to touch the toes at the height of the split.

Learning individual dance steps is not the whole of dancing, however. Once Eddie had mastered the steps he practiced putting them together in combinations. These were short at first but grew longer and more difficult until he could dance a complete solo part such as The Miller in "The Three-Cornered Hat" or Harlequin in "Carnival."

While his muscles were being retrained and repatterned to respond spontaneously to musical rhythms, his mind was also being trained. Although people in the audience seldom realize it, dancing requires a disciplined mind. "A memory that an FBI agent would envy," as dancer-author Agnes de

Mille has said. In a studio classroom, the teacher will demonstrate a solo part from a standard ballet while students watch. Eyes record the movements and memory stores the patterns which are made with each bar of music. Then the student, in turn, produces the same steps and gestures while the pianist repeats the music for him.

Learning all the steps in the right combinations and sequence for just one fifteen-minute ballet takes tremendous concentration. A student who hopes to become a professional, dancing with a ballet company or on television or in movies, must learn not just one ballet but a dozen or more. He never knows when he may be called on to dance a cowboy, a gypsy, a prince, or a sailor—to symphonic music or jazz. He must be master of them all if he expects to be accepted as a salaried member of a top ballet company.

When Eddie began taking lessons again at the School of American Ballet, he hoped that he was headed for a professional dance career. The school is associated with the New York City Ballet Company, and many dancers who take its full course of training and meet its rigorous standards are invited to become members of that company. But no one takes it for granted.

The lucky dance graduate who achieves this goal dances as a member of the corps de ballet of one of the world's top-rated dance groups. Its home is the multimillion-dollar gleaming New York State Theater at Lincoln Center in Manhattan. Costumes, scenic designs, and music are produced by top artists in their fields. Most important, though, its director is George Balanchine, who has created more than 150 ballets as well as dances for musical comedy and the movies. To work in a ballet company directed by Balanchine is the dream of hundreds of young people practicing full time in dance studios all over the country. Eddie Villella, full-time cadet but only part-time dancer, was competing with them for a place in Mr. B.'s company. It was like a boxer climbing into the ring with one hand strapped to his side.

For a year and a half he juggled his duties at Maritime so adroitly that he could slip into town to take lessons. When he went on a summer cruise to Europe he even managed to tuck a ballet practice record into a seabag! Waiting until his bunkmates left the cabin, he would play the record and practice ballet steps until he heard someone coming back.

Finally, in the spring of 1957, he came to a major decision. He could not split his energies this way any longer. With only one semester to go before graduation, he left Maritime and officially joined the New York City Ballet as a member of the corps.

He had been scared walking through the gates of Maritime the first day, but his emotions now were joy and relief, not fear.

"I couldn't believe that I was going to be *paid* for dancing!" he says.

He was at last doing what he was born to do.

Two weeks after joining the company he was given a chance to dance the featured role in two ballets: "The Afternoon of a Faun" and "Souvenirs." The boy who had given up dancing for four years while he studied seamanship and navigation launched his career solidly: The audiences liked him, and so did George Balanchine. Was he scared? "I've never had stage fright," he says. "I was too busy learning the dance roles."

Within a year he was firmly established as a soloist with the company—one of the "most promising young dancers in America," the critics said. They liked his "hurtling, bravura style" and his ability to "bound to a height of six feet while executing spectacular leaps."

"When Eddie Villella dances, manliness comes into ballet," said one reporter.

The New York City Ballet went overseas in 1958 to tour the major cities of Japan and Australia and he danced important roles in both classical and modern ballets.

This kind of solid success with ballet audiences around America and overseas was proof positive that leaving Maritime had been the right thing to do. Dancers are schooled so thoroughly in their own field and undergo such strict discipline they do not have time for formal education. No one ever expected Anna Pavlova or Nijinsky to earn a college degree. And no one expected Eddie Villella to bother about that unfinished semester at Maritime. He could not put it completely out of his mind, though. When the New York City Ballet Company came home to Manhattan early in 1959, he went back to the campus and asked if he could finish. The answer was yes. Carrying a full load as a dancer and a full load as a college student was a grueling business.

"I studied from five until eight every morning, went off to classes until midafternoon, then rushed into town to rehearse and warm up. I danced the evening performance, and finally about 12:30 or one got to bed," he recalls.

Living on four hours of sleep a night was taking a toll of his energies and he says frankly that he would have collapsed "if I'd had to do it two weeks longer." Yet, he adds proudly, "My grades were the highest of all my semesters at Maritime: 3.6. I wanted the degree. I was concentrating."

Ed Villella had set stiff goals for himself in two vastly different fields and managed, through savage determination and by pushing himself to the absolute limit of endurance, to reach them. At this point he might easily have decided it was time to concentrate just on dancing—and his personal life. He was engaged to marry Janet Greschler, also a dancer in the New York City Ballet, and they were making plans for their wedding.

But his ambition and creative energies could not be narrowly channeled. No other American dancer has been involved in such an awesome variety of profitable commercial ventures while maintaining his status as a classical dancer. He is president of a group of discothèques. He has appeared in the musical comedy *Brigadoon* several times, has danced regularly on television on the *Ed Sullivan Show* and *The Bell Telephone Hour,* and was the subject of an hour-long TV documentary, *Man Who Dances: Edward Villella.*

To make the documentary, a camera crew spent months shooting movie footage of him rehearsing, learning new roles, warming up with Patricia McBride—the ballerina who has most frequently been his partner—and dancing extra assignments when other male dancers were sick, although he was pushing himself so hard that his leg muscles knotted into agonizing cramps.

Finally, the documentary showed him giving a lecture and dance demonstration to high-school students who came primed to jeer a "ballet dancer in goofy clothes" and were amazed to see the ex-boxer, ex-baseball player from Maritime College perform physical feats that even the toughest sports star could not match.

His message to the students—in attitude and action, if not in so many words—was that dancing is just as challenging to a man as any other occupation. It happens to demand tremendous discipline . . . but to someone like Eddie Villella, who has talent and accepts the discipline, it also offers tremendous rewards.

"I'm a lucky guy, doing what I love and making a good living out of it," he says. "I feel privileged to be me."

"To live is to dance, to dance is to live," says Snoopy. It sums up what Edward Villella believes with all his heart.

"I Feel Like a Retread, Going Back to School"

Carl Stokes

In the cabin of the big plane, a signal flashed on: FASTEN SEAT BELTS.

"Are we going to land soon?" young Carl asked.

Carl Stokes smiled down at his son.

"We'll be in El Paso Airport in about five minutes."

Across the aisle, five-year-old Cordi squirmed in the seat beside her mother.

"Is it as big as Cleveland?" she asked her father.

He explained that it was a bit smaller.

"But people here can vote for you," Cordi insisted.

Eight-year-old Carl gave his sister a disgusted look. "No, they can't! Only people in Cleveland can vote for Dad. Down here in Texas they vote for their own mayors—each different town does. Dad can't get elected down here."

Dad can't get elected down here.

Young Carl's explanation was simple and straightforward enough to satisfy his sister. But to his father the words had a much deeper—more painful—meaning.

Even if he had been a resident of El Paso, Carl Stokes almost certainly could not have been elected—or even nominated—here. Though Negroes had made progress in sports, business, and the arts, it was unrealistic for a Negro candidate to run for mayor of a major city in the South this fall of 1967.

But how about his chances in Cleveland? Could Carl Stokes become mayor in his own city?

He had just taken the first giant step toward his goal by winning the primary election on the Democratic ticket a few days before. It had been a tough, three-way race: Stokes against Ralph Locher, the incumbent mayor, and another candidate, Frank Celeste. The victory against the other Democrats had been impressive. Final returns showed 110,552 for Stokes, 92,321 for Locher, and only 8509 for the third candidate.

Now he was taking a short rest with his wife's family in Texas. In a week he would go back to Cleveland to face a challenge even stiffer than the primary's: defeating the Republican candidate, Seth C. Taft, grandson of the twenty-seventh President of the United States and the bearer of an illustrious name in Ohio politics.

Many of the people—"Stokes' Folks" as they called themselves—young and old, black and white, who had helped him win the primary by collecting money, some of it nickels and dimes saved by the poor in Mason jars, and ringing doorbells to remind people to register were sure he could do it. Carl Stokes would be the first Negro mayor of any large city in the United States.

They argued that he had made a strong try for mayor in 1965, just two years before. Cleveland's Mayor Locher had been his opponent then too. And Stokes had lost by only 2100 votes. If he could come that close to his goal in '65, he was sure to go over the top in '67, they assured him.

Carl Stokes was grateful for their loyalty and their high hopes. But he knew he had a tough race ahead. Cleveland was a troubled city and the voters were tense.

In the summer of 1966, Cleveland had been wracked by riots. As in many American cities where tensions were high between Negroes and whites, fighting had broken out between police and people in the sweltering inner city.

When the riots were over, a great many Clevelanders were fiercely determined to elect Carl Stokes, a highly respected lawyer and state representative, as their next mayor.

But others were just as fiercely determined to defeat him. Almost 100,000 people—most of them white—had voted against him in the primary election. If he was to win in November he had to persuade a good many of them that he would be a mayor who worked not just for the good of Negroes but of all Clevelanders.

The big plane banked for its landing at El Paso. Carl Stokes closed his eyes a moment, trying to shut out the rhythmic thrum of the motors.

For a week he and his wife, Shirley, and the children would rest and relax. Then he would go back to Cleveland to make the last big push. He would be campaigning sixteen hours a day speaking to Polish-American clubs and fund-raising dinner parties in exclusive Shaker Heights. He would be debating Seth Taft at the City Club and greeting well-wishers at the Greater Abyssinia Baptist Church.

Wherever he went he had to make sure that people understood that he was a moderate, not a militant, and that he loved his city and knew its problems as only a boy who had grown up in the Cleveland slums could know them.

"Paper, mister?"

The bleary-eyed man in a torn shirt looked down at young Carl Stokes and grunted drunkenly. "No money, kid." He staggered to a stop beside a newsstand where eight-year-old Carl and his older brother Louis sometimes sold papers.

"Wha's news?" the man asked thickly.

Carl scanned the headlines.

"It's about President Roosevelt. He may come to Cleveland."

" 'S good. 'N he'll give us all jobs?"

The boy shook his head. "Even the President can't do that."

"Somebody gotta do some'n," the man muttered. " 'S bad!"

Carl watched him stagger away. Even though his mind

was muddled with alcohol, the man had spoken the truth. Times were bad. The year was 1935 and it was no better than all the other years that Carl could remember.

America was in the grip of the great depression that had started in 1929, when Carl was two years old. The giant iron foundries and steel mills in Cleveland that meant work for the Poles, Hungarians, Ukrainians, and other hardworking Americans of Balkan origin were laying off more and more men daily.

For Negro families, times were especially bad. Everywhere in Central, the section where the Stokes boys lived with their widowed mother, families tried desperately to earn enough money for food and rent. Fathers left their tenement homes before daybreak to go down to the hiring halls on Lake Erie and wait in line for hours hoping to be called for a job—any job, paying any wages at all.

Mothers like Louise Stokes left their children in the care of a grandmother or aged aunt so they could go out and earn a few dollars washing clothes or cleaning at the middle-class homes across the Cuyahoga River in Cleveland's West Side.

"I'll give you $1.50 for the day," was what most housewives on the West Side said when a cleaning woman asked for work. Sometimes, if she was lucky, it was $1.75 with a dime or two for carfare at night back home across the river to Central.

But for Louise Stokes and other cleaning women, earning that money meant eight or nine hours of backbreaking labor: washing clothes for a whole family in a tub in the basement; beating rugs hung over a clothesline in the backyard; scrubbing floors on hands and knees.

Years of work like this left Mrs. Stokes "with knuckles as big as knots," Carl said when he was a grown man.

On days when Mrs. Stokes was lucky enough to get work, she got up at dawn, fixed tea and bread for her breakfast, and left before the boys were awake. She was always careful to put bread away in a box with a tight lid. Rats lived in the walls and crawled out to steal food if even a scrap was left on the table.

Slum rats didn't intimidate Louise Stokes. She had acquired enough quiet courage over the years even to cope with them, the boys found.

"Don't be afraid," she told them. "We'll be all right. They won't hurt us."

"But they're big, Mom!" Louis would protest.

"Not as big as we are! We'll seal up the holes and keep them out."

Working together, they managed to keep the ratholes patched and their cramped bedroom as clean and neat as possible. But it took constant work.

The boys didn't think about rats when they were at school or out in the neighborhood doing odd jobs to make money. But at night when Carl and Louis were in bed and the tenement had quieted down they heard them rustling and scuttling behind the cardboard-thin walls of their room.

Sometimes when young Carl huddled close to his brother in bed at night he wondered if things would ever be better. It hurt him to have his mother leave so early in the morning and come home bone-tired at night.

Would the depression never end? Sometimes on hot nights when men on the block sat outside on the front stoops they said that if the big steel mills and iron foundries would open again and start hiring, people could have regular jobs. There would be money for rent and food. Times would be good again.

"It was like that once," Carl's grandmother assured him. "Ten years ago, back around 1927, when you were born, times were good. Your father was working in a laundry and made a pretty good salary."

But Charles Stokes had died in 1929 and to support herself and her two young sons Louise Stokes had had to find work in a city paralyzed by unemployment.

Listening to these stories of his family made Carl wonder

whether things would get better. Would life always be hard for them?

"Not if you study," his mother declared. "If you study, you've got to amount to something!"

Louise Stokes had faith in books. A book was the one gift she somehow managed to buy for each of the boys' birthdays. It wasn't a fancy one—just something printed on cheap paper and cardboard-bound. The five-and-ten had them on the counter, titles like *Five Little Peppers*.

She encouraged the boys to borrow books from the library too. Carl was not an avid reader, but he did go sometimes to look around for a book with action. He was careful, though, not to walk home with it in plain sight. Central was a tough neighborhood and the boys on his block would have roughed him up if they had seen him with a book. So when he got close to home he slipped it under his shirt. It was his business if he wanted to read a library book once in a while —and Carl figured he'd keep it that way.

The one big thing in his life at that point wasn't really books. It was boxing. Joe Louis, the Negro heavyweight champion, was his hero. When Louis was fighting at Madison Square Garden in New York, young Carl hunched beside the radio listening to every word of the broadcast.

He had power, that Louis! There were pictures and stories of him in the papers all the time, and when Carl was selling papers he read about Joe in the sports pages. Sometimes when Lou Stokes felt like it, the brothers would trade punches for practice.

"Watch this right cross," Carl would say.

"Too slow!" Lou would answer, dancing away.

Lou could bob and weave faster than his kid brother could throw punches and he made Carl feel that he'd never "shape up." But there were other boys on the block who were just Carl's age and size and were willing to spar with him, and he was a good match for them.

Boxing was just a way to have fun—at first. As he entered his teens and developed skill, though, Carl began to feel confident. He was learning how to handle himself, how to duck a punch and land a jab when he had to. He'd probably never be a champ like Joe Louis, never have his name in the papers or be interviewed on the radio. No use dreaming about things that ambitious. . . .

But even an amateur could get much out of boxing. Carl's muscles were firming up. His reflexes were fast and he moved like a panther. The word was getting around the neighborhood, too, that you had better not rough him up. When you lived in a section like Central, that was important. There were plenty of toughs there. And the only kids they let alone were ones like Carl Stokes who knew what to do with their fists.

Years later he told a news reporter, "All of us in Central looked on boxing as a way of life. We *had* to fight!"

In September, 1941, when Carl was 14, he entered East Technical High School. The United States was coming out of the depression, and Cleveland had entered a new period of prosperity. Iron and steel were needed in great quantities for the ships that America was sending to England in its fight against Hitler. The city's foundries were operating at full force. In December, when the Japanese bombed Pearl Harbor, and America declared war against Japan and Germany, the tempo was stepped up. Factories that had been operating at full employment on two shifts went to three. The skies over the city were red at night from the reflection of the blast furnaces. "Help Wanted" signs were out at all the factories along the Cuyahoga.

Carl was restless. After two years at East Technical, he begged his mother to let him drop out of school and go to work. He could count on making a few dollars a week by running errands and doing other part-time jobs for storekeepers, but this was trifling compared to the salaries his teenage friends were getting in the factories.

"Jobs on the block are baby stuff," he told his mother.

"I'm grateful for them, just the same!"

"But I want a good job—something that pays real money."

"You're only sixteen, Carl," she reminded him. "If you study and finish school you'll be somebody someday."

Someday. It seemed far off.

He went back to school for one more year. But in the summer of 1944, when he was seventeen, he made up his mind that he had all the schooling he would ever need. He applied for a job at a factory, was hired, and when September came did not go back to East Technical.

For almost a year he worked at the foundry, but again he grew restless. Several of his friends were in the service and, shortly after his eighteenth birthday, he enlisted in the Army. The year was 1945 and Hitler's forces had been defeated. American soldiers who had fought in Europe were being shipped home and fresh young troops from the States were taking their place in the army of occupation. One of the young soldiers assigned to Germany was Private Carl Burton Stokes.

Army life in this period was not hard: Food was plain but plentiful, duties were routine, and there was plenty of time for recreation. Carl filled in evenings playing table tennis and perfected a scorching serve and slashing backhand that made him champ of the European forces.

He also had a chance to do some boxing in Germany. The punches he had learned back home were adequate but amateurish compared with the technique of the top Army boxers. When Carl wasn't boxing or working out he made a point of watching the Army champs train. One of them impressed him especially. Carl began to ask him questions about technique and before long they were good friends.

"What are you going to do with yourself when you get out of the service?" he asked Carl one day.

Carl's answer was that he would probably go back to Cleveland to another job at a foundry.

"But that's a dead end!"

"I can't get much more," Carl explained. "I quit high school when I was seventeen."

"You can still get your diploma," the friend told him. "Go home and hit the books. You've got brains—don't waste 'em!"

Five months later when his Army duty was over, Carl—by now a corporal—came home to Cleveland and enrolled at East Technical. Getting into the rhythm of studying was hard for him at first, but he stuck to it and a year later had his high-school diploma.

Carl was sure now that he wanted to go to college. He enrolled under the GI bill at West Virginia State College and the following year transferred to Cleveland College of Western Reserve.

"Carl's really settled down this time," his mother told a friend.

It looked that way until the summer after his sophomore year. He took a job as chauffeur for a political organizer in Gov. Frank Lausche's campaign, and he impressed his boss so much that he was encouraged to try for a state job. The Ohio Department of Liquor Control was looking for enforcement agents. They had to be young and able to "handle some tough customers." Carl applied and was accepted.

"When are you going to finish college?" his mother asked.

"Someday, Mom," he told her, "I'll go back and get that diploma. I want to work a year."

The year stretched out. Being a liquor enforcement agent meant checking on saloon and tavern owners in all sections of Cleveland. Most of the calls Stokes made were routine: The owners wanted to keep their licenses, so they abided by state laws. But once in a while a tavern owner had let his license expire or was selling bootleg whiskey. If Stokes made an unexpected visit he had a fight on his hands.

"It's usually somebody throwing a wild punch," he told his brother. "I can handle those. But last week some bootleggers pulled a gun on my partner and me, and we had a shoot-out."

Bar owners in Cleveland began to have respect for the tall (6-foot), lean (150-lb.) inspector who could handle his fists when he had to.

"He looks scrawny, but don't let that fool you," one bar-keeper said. "Nothing gets by this Stokes!"

There were eighty-five inspectors in the department and he had the second highest record of arrests.

The Stokes family, meanwhile, had quietly but persistently been reminding Carl that he had unfinished business —at college. Louis had finished law training and had just passed his exams to practice in the state of Ohio.

"If I can do it, you can do it!" he told his younger brother.

Carl applied to the University of Minnesota and was accepted in the fall of 1952 soon after his twenty-fifth birthday.

"I'm not exactly the youngest guy on campus!" he wrote a friend. "I feel like a retread. But it's good to be back."

As a student majoring in law, he had a "mountain" of books to read every week. But Stokes was determined that his stop-and-go education would be completed this time. He stuck with his studies. He did take a job, but it was for weekends only.

"It gives me a chance to travel," he wrote his mother. "I'm a dining-car waiter on a crack train, the 'Rock Island Rocket.' I go to Dallas and back to Minneapolis every weekend, and Monday morning I'm back in class."

In 1954, when he was twenty-seven, Carl graduated from college with a Bachelor of Science degree in law.

"What are your plans now?" his mother asked.

He told her that he had a chance to be a probation officer for the Cleveland Municipal Court.

". . . and I might do a little more studying. Maybe some evening courses so I can pass the state bar exam."

For the next two years while he worked days checking on men and boys who were out of jail on probation he attended night classes at Cleveland-Marshall Law School to earn his LL.B. degree. The following year, when he was thirty, he passed the exam and qualified to practice law in his home state.

The day Carl passed the bar exams Louis told him, "You're resigning your court job—right now! I'm not practicing law alone anymore. You and I are forming a new firm, 'Stokes and Stokes.' "

Building on the law practice that Louis had started, the brothers expanded their list of clients and soon began representing prominent businessmen, Negro and white. Within a year Cleveland's Mayor Anthony Celebrezze appointed Carl an assistant city prosecutor. His boss in the new appointment was Ralph Locher, the man he would challenge within four years for the post of mayor of Cleveland.

The year 1958 was important to him for another, very different reason. He married slim, attractive Shirley Edwards, a graduate in library science from Fisk University, Nashville.

He was beginning to take an interest in local politics and became a member of the Democratic party's executive committee in Cuyahoga County, which includes Cleveland. By 1962 he felt he was ready to launch a career in politics: He campaigned for the state legislature and won, becoming the first Negro Democrat ever to sit in the Ohio State House of Representatives.

Almost everywhere he went, Stokes was hearing lawyers and businessmen say that Cleveland was beginning to slip. The chamber of commerce had long boasted proudly that Cleveland was "The Best Location in the Nation." But it was clear to a lot of people that this was no longer true. The factories centered in the heart of the city along the Cuyahoga River were running below peak levels and unemployment was a growing problem, especially among unskilled workers. To unemployed Negroes in sections like Hough and Glenville, Cleveland was not "The Best Location in the Nation," but "The Mistake on the Lake."

"What this town needs is new blood, new thinking from some energetic young men," business leaders were saying. "The next mayor of Cleveland has to put us back into competition with other towns so we can attract new industry."

One name was mentioned oftener than any others: Rep. Carl Stokes.

"He's a good man but too young," said some.

"He's a good man and 300,000 Negro people in Cleveland will vote for him—but how about the whites?" said others.

At the Lancer Restaurant on Carnegie Avenue, influential Negro businessmen considered other names during the summer of 1965. But they always came back to Carl Stokes. In late summer they approached him. He agreed to be a candidate and picked a prominent Negro surgeon, Dr. Kenneth Clement, as his campaign manager.

Petitions were circulated to get enough signatures so that he could run as an independent Democrat without having to enter the primary race against Mayor Ralph Locher, also a Democrat.

"Stokes hasn't got a chance," skeptics said. Other Clevelanders, including veteran newsmen, were saying that it just might be a close election. They were right: Stokes lost by 2100 votes.

"What are you going to do now?" his wife asked.

"Tomorrow morning," he told her, "I'm starting to work on the '67 election."

Carefully, month by month for the next year and a half, he and Doctor Clement put together an organization of Negroes and whites, Polish- and Italian-Americans, college professors and truck drivers. All ethnic groups—and all levels of income and education—were represented in the "Stokes' Folks" volunteers.

The campaign needed broad-based support from Cleveland leaders and it came, in a trickle at first and then in a flood. Thomas Vail, publisher of the Cleveland *Plain Dealer*, announced that his paper would support Stokes. Cyrus

Eaton, millionaire industrialist, offered his help. George Herzog, a director of twenty-three corporations, volunteered to serve as campaign treasurer.

Businessmen who lived in spacious homes in Shaker Heights asked their wives to give dinner parties so that white Clevelanders could meet Carl and Shirley Stokes and judge for themselves whether he was the kind of man they wanted as mayor of Cleveland.

He quietly repeated to them what he had told a group of Hungarian-Americans earlier: "When I ran for mayor in '65 people whispered all over the West Side and the South Side that I was a Negro. Well, they don't have to whisper it in this campaign. I am a Negro. I'm proud of it. I intend to remain one."

Whether he talked in private homes to small groups or in high-school auditoriums to large, Carl Stokes kept emphasizing that he should be judged not on his race but on his personal qualifications. His voting record as a state representative proved him to be a moderate, not a militant who favored Negroes over whites.

But many people were hard to convince. One rally, packed with outspoken opponents, was so tense that his backers were afraid of what would happen when he stepped onstage. He assured them quietly that everything would be all right. He then walked onstage, smiled, and said, "I really don't have anything to tell you people. I just came here so you could see that I don't have horns and a tail!"

A woman said later, "It was magic. It broke the tension. Expressions changed immediately. You could see they were at least willing to listen."

While he was campaigning day and night on the West Side to win white voters, his backers were working in the poor neighborhoods across the river, going from door to door reminding Negroes to register.

"You've got to register if you want to vote in the October primary and in November," they told them.

The primary election to pick the Democratic candidate

among the three challengers was held the first week in October. When the votes were counted Carl Stokes had won by 18,000 votes. It was at this point that he decided to take his wife, son, and daughter to Texas for a rest and a visit with his wife's family.

Meanwhile, at campaign headquarters on the ground floor of the Rockefeller Building in Cleveland, Doctor Clement began analyzing the primary vote. He wanted to be sure that the victory in October against Mayor Locher and the other challenger would be followed by victory in November against the Republican candidate, Seth Taft.

When the visit to Texas was over and Stokes flew back to Cleveland, campaign strategy for November had been plotted down to the smallest detail. Some 600 college students had volunteered to go out knocking on doors in all parts of the city, passing out literature. A telethon to raise funds was being launched under a young Army communications expert who had just returned from Vietnam. Advertising men were writing newspaper ads and "Vote for Stokes" spots for television.

Upstairs in the Rockefeller Building in a room marked "No Admittance," an expert accountant studied tabletop computers which clicked out predictions. As information was fed into them they calculated what the vote on November 8 would be.

In mid-October the prediction was one that made his volunteers grin: Stokes leading Taft by a big margin. Taft proved to be a rugged campaigner during the last weeks, however. On November 6, two days before Cleveland voters would go to the polls, the Stokes lead was down to less than one percent.

On Tuesday morning, November 8, the skies over Cleveland were bleak and snow was falling. Bad weather usually means a light turnout, but radio news reporters began announcing by midmorning that voters were flocking to the polls.

Early returns from the West Side showed by evening that

thousands of white Democrats had rejected their party candidate to vote for Republican Taft. Throughout the evening young volunteers who had worked hard on the campaign came down to headquarters to watch returns clicking in. As Taft votes continued to pile up, they grew tense.

At midnight, news announcers on all stations were saying bluntly that there was a definite "tide toward Taft."

"It looks bad," said one young volunteer under his breath.

"We're not giving up yet!" another answered fiercely.

Soon after 1 A.M. returns began coming in from the East Side and for the first time, Stokes began inching ahead. Within an hour it was official: Seth Taft, 127,328 votes; Carl Stokes, 129,829. He had won by 2501 votes.

The crowd at headquarters exploded. They threw hats into the air and cheered jubilantly. A Dixieland band played as black volunteers and white slapped one another on the back and shouted, "We've got ourselves a mayor!" and "We made it!"

Minutes later, police cleared an aisle through the packed room, and Carl Stokes, tightly gripping the hand of his wife, appeared and a roar went up. He was lifted to the stage and appealed for quiet.

"I want to thank you—all of you—for this victory," he told them. "The Poles, Slovenians, Italians, Negroes, everybody in Cleveland who made this possible. Never before tonight have I known the true meaning of the words 'God bless America,' but I know them now. . . ."

After more thanks, he and his wife left for another victory celebration at the Cleveland-Sheraton Hotel. Shortly after 3 A.M. Seth Taft and his wife called at the hotel. As Mrs. Taft handed Mrs. Stokes a box of long-stemmed roses, Taft warmly shook hands and congratulated the man who had defeated him.

The newsboy from the slums of Central who dropped out of school to work in a foundry and serve in the Army had become the fiftieth mayor of Cleveland, Ohio.

"There's No Feeling in the World Like This . . . ."

Peggy Fleming

The crowd in the packed Cleveland Arena leaned forward expectantly as the loudspeaker announced the name of the next skater: Peggy Fleming. It was the final night of competition for the 1964 United States figure-skating title, and a slim fifteen-year-old girl from California was going into the last event with hopes of being picked for the U. S. Olympic team.

If she could present a four-minute program of free skating —leaps, spins, pirouettes that were perfectly coordinated to music—the judges might give her the points she needed to do the impossible—defeat the reigning champion and become U. S. Senior Women's titleholder.

Two days before, Peggy and the other finalists had completed the grueling first part of the tests, skating the compulsory figures. These are intricate patterns that have to be traced and retraced with absolute precision. When the panel of judges had gone down on hands and knees to examine the tracings made by each skater they ranked Peggy in third place behind Lorraine Hanlon, the seventeen-year-old champion who was fighting to keep her title, and another contender.

If Peggy was to come from behind and pass these two, her free skating would have to be spectacular. Skating awkwardly or out of rhythm or taking a bad fall on the ice would bring the final tally down disastrously.

As she waited at rinkside for her music to start, she glanced at the figure of her father standing with a group of parents and coaches. He smiled and winked. Then she scanned the balcony, hoping to see her mother. These two, Albert and Doris Fleming, had driven all the way from California to see their daughter compete.

"Dad'll be downstairs to lend a hand if you need him," Mrs. Fleming had told her, "and I'll be up in the balcony. I know you'll come through your free skating with a good fat score!"

The strains of "Prima Ballerina" floated out through the Arena, and Peggy skimmed onto the ice, blending her strokes to the lilt of the music, letting it carry her into glides, turns, spins. Applause rippled through the crowd and she began skating now with assurance. The cold ache she always felt in the last seconds before going onto the ice was gone. She was feeling the strains of the music and letting it carry her rhythmically. Leaps, jumps, then the final spin—fast—and it was over!

The crowd loved it. Wave after wave of applause followed her as she left the ice.

"Nice job," said one of the skaters at rinkside. It was the guarded comment that always came after free skating. But what would the judges say? Standing beside her father, Peggy waited for the scoring to be completed. On all sides were other young skaters, some sweating out the decision alone, others with a parent. Shortly before 10 o'clock the totals were announced: The new United States Senior Women's Figure Skating Champion was Peggy Fleming of Pasadena, California!

With a whoop of joy her father lifted her high in the air. "You did it, Peg! You did it," he exulted, hugging her fiercely. "Cleveland was good luck, wasn't it?"

A reporter asked for an explanation.

"Cleveland is special to Peg," Mr. Fleming said with a broad smile. "This is where she learned to skate—here at the Arena—when she was nine years old."

It was Albert Fleming who bought Peggy her first pair of skates. She had gone skating with her older sister Janice a short time before and had glided around the rink with amazing ease. It seemed such a good outlet for her abundant energies that her father bought the skates and enrolled her in a class.

Doris Fleming approved the idea heartily. She, her husband, and their four daughters had moved to an apartment in Cleveland from a ranch in San Jose, California, early that year—1958—so that Albert Fleming could learn newspaper color printing. For three of the girls—Janice, ten; Maxine, seven; and little Cathy, three—the move meant only minor adjustments: getting to know new teachers and making new friends. But for Peggy, the Flemings' energetic nine-year-old, apartment living meant confinement. The running, jumping, tree climbing she loved in California had to give place to urban pastimes: dressing dolls and playing hopscotch in front of the apartment house. She was restless and had begun teasing Janice and Maxine.

When the girls complained to their mother she reminded them that Peggy was not a mean child—"it's just that she has a lot of Irish in her."

Keeping peace among her daughters would be easier, Doris Fleming told her husband, if they could find something—a hobby, perhaps—that Peggy liked.

It occurred to him that ice-skating was a possibility. It was a good healthful sport; it was fun; and he had heard that the skating classes at the Arena were an excellent way for a child to get instruction in the basics. Of course, Peggy might not like skating. But Albert Fleming was hopeful. He loved all sports himself, and his little "mick" of a daughter might take to it.

Even if she acquired only enough skill to go round and round the Arena rink, at least it was a nice ladylike sport, he reasoned.

Lessons began on a Saturday afternoon, and Peggy discovered to her delight that she liked everything about them. Several children complained of weak ankles, but Peggy's skates felt just right for her; if most of the others wobbled

along, she glided. The teacher was good-natured and patient, and taking lessons from her was almost like playing
follow-the-leader.

She explained to her class of beginners that they would
never enjoy skating if they were tense—if they went out on
the ice with rigid backs and stiff arms. One of the first rules
to remember was to keep the knees "soft."

"Don't tense up," she said. "You're going to fall on the ice
plenty of times—everyone does, even Olympic champions.
But it's not as hard as falling on a sidewalk. Ice is slippery
and you'll slip *with* it to cushion your fall. Just pick yourself
up and go on skating. Relax when you're out here on the ice
and enjoy it."

For Peggy that was easy. She had never enjoyed anything
as much as this new game. Her father called it a sport and
spoke of it with a kind of respect. But for this nine-year-old
it was a fascinating game. Each lesson was more exciting
than the last. She loved the clean expanse of ice and moving
through the cool air with quick, free strokes.

For many of the beginners, balancing the body on a single blade of steel was a torturous business. She saw classmates clump out to the ice and wobble painfully around
with arms flailing and faces contorted. Peggy felt sorry for
them. The ice was their enemy. It terrified them.

Skating came so easily to Peggy that within a month she
had mastered the basics and was learning the "edges" that
are the important first step to figure skating. An edge results
from a leaning of the entire body to one side or the other so
that the metal skate cuts the ice not with the flat of the
blade but with either the inside or outside edge. When a
skater traces a circle eight on the ice, for instance, he must
be able to skate inside and outside edges on the right or left
foot, forward and backward.

The teachers at the Cleveland Arena said that figure skating was almost like "drawing" a pattern on ice with the
body, using the blade as the pen point. Peggy was delighted

to discover how much more accurate her figure work became with practice.

"I'm doing three-turns and serpentines," she told her surprised parents one day. "And in two weeks I'm going to try my preliminary test."

It was a new language for the Fleming family and a bit confusing at first. To find out what three-turns and serpentines were, Mr. Fleming began stopping off at the Arena to watch Peggy practice whenever he could spare time from his newspaper training. Standing at rinkside watching his slim, freckle-faced daughter go through the basic figures, he began to understand the techniques of the sport. Peggy was having some trouble with the backward edges, but it amazed him that this nine-year-old had mastered everything else in just a short time.

His words to her when she came off the rink were always encouraging: "You're on your way, Peg. You're going to be a fine skater someday."

Her progress was so good that she was able to pass both the preliminary and the "First" tests of the U. S. Figure Skating Association just two and a half months after starting lessons.

"It was fun!" she said when the tests were over. "We had to do the waltz eight, four rolls, the inside and outside forward eight and some others. We couldn't have wobbles or flats. And no toe pushes!"

With these tests behind her, Peggy began planning for the U. S. Figure Skating Association's "Second." Her teacher at the Arena had explained that once skaters get safely past the "prelim" and the First, the Association expects them to train for future hurdles; i.e., the seven proficiency exams leading up to the extremely difficult "Eighth" or "Gold Medal" test—comparable to the Black Belt in karate.

It was shortly after this that Peggy's days of skating at the Arena came to an end. Mr. Fleming's training period at the Cleveland newspaper was over and he had taken a job in

San Francisco. The family returned to the West Coast and Peggy began skating in Berkeley.

Again she took lessons and, working systematically, began to perfect first one and then another of the compulsory figures that are the basis for all advanced and even championship skating competition.

"Practice the eights, practice the eights!" she heard her teacher say again and again. The instructors Peggy had met in Cleveland and in Berkeley stressed this mastery of the basics. Cutting a perfect figure eight is as important to a skater, they said, as practicing scales is to a pianist.

With Peggy at the rink that season of 1958 and again in 1959 were other novices working to pass their Second and Third tests—and asking constantly about competing. She, too, was anxious to match her skills against the field. Her parents thought she was good and her teachers were encouraging. But how would she rate when skating against other really talented juveniles?

In the winter of 1959, when Peggy was ten years old, her teacher finally agreed that she was ready for competition. She entered the Juvenile Girls' division of the Central Pacific competition at San Francisco—and took first place.

Her parents were overjoyed. Veteran skaters who had hinted that little Peg Fleming was a "natural" were right, after all.

To Peggy herself, winning this title the first time she competed was a heady experience—and scary too. When you're ten years old and have all those judges watching with owlish eyes while you do your figures, you're bound to be nervous. But winning a title wasn't *too* hard. . . .

"If you can do that well the first time you compete, you ought to be a top winner next month again," one of the skaters told her.

Peggy disagreed—but not too strenuously. To her ears, the prediction didn't sound farfetched at all.

Six weeks later the Pacific Coast championships were held

in Los Angeles. The girl who had breezed to a first in San Francisco came in twelfth. Dead last.

It was a sobering experience and one that stayed with her a long time. Years later when she was an Olympic champion she candidly admitted that she had trained for this second competition much more lazily than for the first. Many of the girls who finished far behind her in San Francisco beat her easily.

"I guess I wasn't trying hard enough," she confessed to her parents.

"We can do something about that!" her father announced.

In the weeks that followed, Peggy discovered that her father did, indeed, mean "we." He worked out a practice schedule calling for cooperation from the whole family. The alarm clock at the Fleming house went off at 5 A.M. Albert Fleming, first out of bed, woke Peggy and got breakfast ready. Mrs. Fleming was up next, packing lunches and getting Janice, Maxine, and Cathy ready for school. By 6 o'clock Peggy was in the family car with her father on the way to the ice rink. As they dashed out the door, Mrs. Fleming called off the checklist of things Peggy would need for practice: skates, guards, practice dress, stockings, gloves.

Schoolbooks and homework rarely went along on this crack-of-dawn trip. They were left at home and Mrs. Fleming stowed them in the car at 7:45, when she drove to the rink to pick Peggy up and take her to school.

Many parents would have considered getting out of the house at this hour too demanding. But Albert Fleming was a determined man. He was sure that these extra hours of practice would pay dividends. After a night's sleep, Peggy's energy was high, and she had the deserted rink to herself so she could concentrate on cutting school figures to perfection.

Even the condition of the ice came under Mr. Fleming's

scrutiny. If it was cut up by blade marks, he would start the resurfacing machine to give Peggy a perfectly clear sheet of ice. When she skimmed over the surface, the figures she cut with the steel blades of her skates shone with sparkling clarity. Every push-off, sending her body swinging into a symmetrical circle, left its mark. Every shift of weight from right to left foot and from inside edge to outside was indelibly imprinted on the clear surface. A push-off that was uncertain, or a wobble as she leaned into the figure, showed up dramatically. Alone with her father in the silent rink, she could study these prints in the ice and read her strengths and weaknesses.

Slowly and methodically she stroked out the school figures: inside forward eight, outside forward eight, inside backward eight, outside backward eight. Were the lobes of the circles symmetrical? Were they traced so that they could be evenly divided by an imaginary axis?

They had to be perfect. They *would* be perfect, Peggy told herself, if she just kept practicing this way, early in the morning with her father there at rinkside. She was determined she was not going to rank dead last in the next competition.

In the winter of 1961, skating in one competition after another, she placed in the top three in all of them and won the Pacific Coast Novice Ladies' Championship. It was time for twelve-year-old Peggy to take a giant step. She had been moving up in the "age ranks" in regional competition—the pattern that every skating hopeful follows. She was ready now to try for a national title.

She entered the Novice Ladies' U. S. competition in the winter of 1962 and placed second. This kind of showing against the best novice skaters in the country convinced her parents that she had championship potential. Would she be another Tenley Albright or Carol Heiss and win national and Olympic honors? Possibly. But she would have to practice —and bide her time.

"We don't want Peg to try for the U. S. 'Senior' too soon,"

her parents were told. Veteran skaters suggested a timetable that would give her an opportunity for "seasoning." If she was patient and remained in West Coast competition until she was sixteen or so, she might have a good chance to take the U. S. Senior Championship.

It sounded reasonable. But Peggy was a young girl in a hurry. She had made an unusual bet with her father: She would be U. S. champion before he broke 80 in golf. How could she win the bet if she was overly cautious?

In the winter of 1963 she competed for the first time in a senior division and won—at age fourteen—the Pacific Coast Senior Ladies' Championship. Still the experts said, "Go slow." Peggy would be foolish, they insisted, to compete in the senior division of the national championships. She would be facing competitors who were sixteen and seventeen years old and had been skating ten years or more.

She had skill, but she was not mature enough—not poised enough . . . so they said.

Peggy talked it over with her parents. She had to make a decision promptly. The 1964 national championships were to be held during the month of January in Cleveland—at the Arena, her home rink.

"Go for the senior division," her mother said.

"I think you can take it," her father told her. "I'm so sure of it that your mother and I are both going to Cleveland to be with you."

The first-day registration at the Arena was a noisy, hectic business. Crowding into the lobby were skaters from all parts of the country: boys and girls who, like Peggy, had successfully competed in regional tests and were now skaters of rank. The boys joked and the girls chattered. Lorraine Hanlon, the seventeen-year-old who was defending champion, arrived and was warmly greeted.

A newspaper reporter, sent out to the Arena to get a feature story, shouldered his way through the high-voltage crowd to the side of an official.

"You couldn't get *me* out on the ice with people watching

how I did spins and jumps. These kids are brave. Don't they ever get jittery?" he asked.

"Visit the locker room the last night," the other answered. "You'll see jitters then. That's when the tension really gets to them!"

Peggy Fleming walked out to rinkside and stared up at the rows of empty seats. Every day for the next week they would be packed with people watching the best skaters in America try to unseat the champions—or defend their crowns. Six years ago she had sat on a bench here at the Arena lacing on skates for the first time. Had she learned enough, practiced hard enough to be United States champion?

You can do it.

Her parents said it quietly that night at the hotel and each day that followed as the competitors went through the complex school figures that accounted for 60 per cent of the total score. By Friday, the official point count showed Peggy in third place. The title would be won or lost the next day when each finalist presented her four-minute program of free skating to music.

The Arena was packed on Saturday evening. As Peggy waited at rinkside she glanced at her father. He smiled and winked. Somewhere in the balcony her mother was watching.

"Peggy Fleming." The name was blurted out of the loudspeaker, and the first measures of "Prima Ballerina" floated through the Arena. Onto the ice she glided. She had four minutes to prove that she was the best woman skater in America. . . .

A little before 10 o'clock, the judges announced their decision: Peggy Fleming was the new U. S. champion. With a shout of joy Albert Fleming swept her into his arms. Reporters crowded in on them, firing questions: Where had she learned to skate? Who were her coaches? Did she have a routine for practice? How? . . . Why? . . . When? . . .

Flashbulbs flared as press photographers moved in. *Let's*

have one more, Miss Fleming . . . over here with your parents. Mrs. Fleming, you were sitting in the balcony? "I was up there saying a prayer." *Were you surprised when your daughter won?* "I was shocked." . . .

The girl who had progressed rapidly through the ranks of regional competition to take the national title was now, by virtue of her championship, on the brink of world competition. The Winter Olympics of 1964 was to open at Innsbruck, Austria, the following month. As U. S. champion, Peggy was made a member of the team.

It was a team that had heart but not much else. Three years before, on February 16, 1961, a tragic airplane crash near Brussels, Belgium, had taken the lives of eighteen champion figure skaters. The replacements who went to Innsbruck that February, 1964, were mostly skaters new to international competition. The coaches, the news reporters, and the general public agreed that the United States could not expect to make much of a showing.

Peggy's youth and natural shyness made her feel the greenest of all the green contenders. When she arrived in Innsbruck and saw the poised skaters from Russia, France, Canada, and Germany practice their routines her morale began to sag. They seemed completely at ease in this high-keyed world of continental skating, chattering and joking with one another in two or three languages. If they were bothered by jitters, they kept it well hidden.

The morning of the free-skating programs, Peggy woke with a sore throat. By the time she reached the ice stadium her head throbbed with fever. On the ice she skated well but uncertainly and took a fall in full view of members of the Royal House of Orange. When the judges announced the totals, Peggy Fleming of the United States ranked sixth.

A few of her teammates said consoling things: "First time skating against the best in the world, Peg. . . ." "A good showing considering the pressure. . . ."

But on the trip home from Innsbruck they blasted her

with rough questions: "What happened to you out there on the ice? Why didn't you win?"

It was almost as if fifteen-year-old Peggy Fleming had personally failed the Olympic team—and 185,000,000 Americans!

If international skating competition was high-pitched and precarious, life at home in Berkeley was solid and stable. Albert and Doris Fleming believed that all four of their daughters should put schoolwork first and then find time for other activities. Janice, the oldest, loved music and could sing Irish ballads in Gaelic. Maxine, third oldest after Peggy, was working for art and citizenship awards. And when Cathy was old enough Mrs. Fleming, who had long been a Brownie leader, introduced her to Girl Scouting.

"What do you all do in your *spare* time?" a classmate once asked Peggy sarcastically.

"We sew!" she shot back. "And we try new hair styles on each other. And we do housework."

"Do you have to do housework?" the girl asked.

"Of course," Peggy answered. "I come home from a trip to Europe, and my sisters say, 'Good to have you back! It's your turn to do the dishes.'"

It was true that she did her share of housework when she was home. But her major energies went into practice at the ice rink for upcoming competitions. In February, 1965, at Lake Placid, New York, she successfully defended her title and won the United States championship for the second straight year. Competing later that month in the North American contests against the best figure skaters of Canada and the U. S., she placed second to Petra Burka of Toronto.

Was she skating at top form? It was clear to Peggy and her parents that she was not. She could have done better if she had not been awed by the more sophisticated contenders.

"I listened to locker-room gossip—and it got to me," she admitted to her parents. "Some of the skaters were taking

me apart. 'Peggy's weak in this. . . . Peggy's weak in that.
. . . Winning the U. S. title when she was fifteen was just a
fluke!' I shouldn't have listened to them—but I did. When I
got out on the ice it stayed with me. They 'psyched' me!"

"What can you do about it?" her mother asked.

"I'm going to be too busy to listen," she said. "I'll read a
magazine or comb my hair—or *something!*"

The following month in Colorado Springs when the
Broadmoor Hotel was host for the World Championships,
Peggy ranked third. She had been skating for years in a rink
where practice time was limited. She did not have the assurance and polish to beat the best women skaters from all
over the world. She was handicapped, also, by having to
skate in the rarefied air of that site.

It seemed to the Flemings that a move from their home in
a smoggy section of California might be good not only for
Peggy but for Albert Fleming as well. He had been fighting
a respiratory weakness, and the doctors had long advised a
change. He resigned his job to take a new one as a press-
man in Colorado Springs and moved the family to a new
home there in June, 1965.

Peggy enrolled at the Cheyenne Mountain High School,
which allows students who are serious skaters to have flexi-
ble programs so they can practice several hours a day.
Equally important, she enrolled at the world-famous Broadmoor Skating Club as a student of Carlo Fassi, the former
European men's skating champion and resident pro at the
club.

If her goal in California had been the U. S. championship,
the goal now in Colorado was the World and—perhaps—the
Olympic championships. To reach it, all the Flemings applied themselves with new determination. Expenses were
skyrocketing: Lessons cost $7 a half hour; in addition, there
was a charge for practice time at the rink—six hours a day,
six days each week!

Peggy also needed skates of the finest quality—$150 a
pair. But Albert and Doris Fleming were able to save on

other expenses. Some skaters expected their parents to buy $150–$200 costumes for them. Mrs. Fleming was sewing Peggy's and doing a professional job—at a fraction of that cost.

"Even Peggy's practice dresses might have cost as much as $25 apiece," she recalled later. "I made 25 to 30 of them a year, plus skirts and slacks for all the girls. They were learning to sew for themselves too. They even made suits."

Newspaper stories had hinted that the Flemings were "struggling" to pay for topflight skating instruction for Peggy.

"They exaggerated when they said 'struggling,'" she explained. "We watched our budget. And in a lot of ways—sewing, for instance—we economized."

At the Broadmoor, skaters of championship caliber were each assigned a "patch"—a strip of ice that was their own for practice at a certain time. By signing up to skate on her patch in the earliest predawn hours, Peggy was able to get it at a low fee.

"When her father couldn't drive Peg, I'd set the alarm for 4:30 some mornings, and we'd be out of the house and at the rink at 5 o'clock," said her mother.

At 5 A.M. in midwinter in the Colorado mountains it is dark—and bitterly cold! Most teen-agers would have considered it torture to leave a warm bed. It was torture for Peggy too. But somehow she learned to grit her teeth and take it as part of training discipline.

Under Carlo Fassi, she was training more intensively than ever. When he first analyzed Peggy's skating technique, he gave her high marks for general skill and especially for free skating. He told her frankly, though, that he was not satisfied with the compulsory figures. "Do them over and over until you have completely mastered them," he told her.

Peggy, often skating with her hair in pigtails at that early hour, would start with slow, simple circles. When she was thoroughly warmed up she would tackle the figures, one at a time. There were forty-eight of them, ranging from the

simple forward eights to the difficult outside and inside forward change-three.

"I spend as much as a half hour on one figure," she told a
magazine reporter that winter. "When I run into trouble I
stay on one even longer. It takes me a week of practice to
get through all forty-eight. Then I begin again."

The requirements for school figures, she explained, are
spelled out almost like a geometric equation. "The positions
of legs, arms, and head—of every part of a skater's body
down to his little fingers—are rigidly specified. And judging
is rough!"

Morning practice lasted until 7 or 7:30. Mrs. Fleming,
who usually waited for Peggy, doing hand sewing in a snug
corner of the rink lobby, would drive her home to relax and
eat a high-protein breakfast: hot cereal, toast, and milk. By
9 o'clock she was back on the ice for more work on the figures and, finally, the part of skating that was pure fun—free
skating to music.

Coach Fassi was conservative in his musical tastes: Music
by the masters—Rossini, Verdi, Tchaikowsky—was best for
free skating, he declared. One morning, on impulse, Peggy
brought a Beatles album from home and played the records
over the Broadmoor amplifiers. The coach listened, then
shrugged and smiled.

"Not bad," he said. "But only here—for practice."

In February, 1966, the U. S. championships were held in
Berkeley, and Peggy won her third straight senior title. Hy-
percritical sports fans had hinted that her first victory two
years before as a fifteen-year-old was a fluke. Some few
were not impressed even by her second championship. But
now even the most skeptical began talking warmly of her
chance to upset Petra Burka of Toronto for the World title.

Petra Burka had defeated Peggy twice in 1965: at the
North American and at the World. She was a highly skilled
skater with keen competitive spirit, but she possessed a de-
lightful personality, and Peggy and she had become close
friends. Three weeks after winning the U. S., Peggy flew to

Davos, Switzerland, for the World. The girls greeted each other warmly and then settled down to the nerve-racking trials.

Compulsory figures came first and Petra amassed 1184.2 points. When Peggy traced and retraced her figures she did them so perfectly that she outpointed her rival with a score of 1233. In the free skating that followed she was judged top winner, thus becoming the first American girl to win the World Championship since Carol Heiss in 1960.

Coach Fassi was ecstatic. The training schedule he had devised had led to victory for his seventeen-year-old pupil. "*Now* you can relax!" he told her. "Forget training, Peg. Enjoy yourself."

With a group of thirty top skaters Peggy started an exhibition tour that took her across Europe to East and West Germany, Austria, England, France and Russia. In Paris she was greeted by Alain Calmat, a former men's world champion, and escorted to champagne dinners at Maxim's, boat tours on the Seine, and sight-seeing at the Eiffel Tower. Strict training rules, followed so carefully for weeks before the World competition, were ignored. This was a time to savor victory by dancing until dawn and eating rich desserts!

After the dazzling Paris-in-the-spring celebration ended, the skaters were to go briefly to Moscow and then home. Peggy's return to Colorado Springs would mean a reunion with her sisters and her father. Mrs. Fleming, who had remained in Europe as a chaperon for the skaters' tour, had heard that there probably would be a parade arranged in Peggy's honor.

But the parade was never given. In the last days of Peggy's stay in Moscow word came suddenly that Albert Fleming had died of a heart attack. Grief-stricken, she flew home immediately—not to a victory celebration but to her father's funeral.

When Albert Fleming died, his wife had to begin planning for the future, considering what would be wise for all her

daughters. She called a family conference and with complete frankness asked her other daughters whether they felt
that Peggy should continue amateur competition.

"We all know how expensive it is," she said. "But your
father and I always felt it was worthwhile—that we were all
enriched. And we've managed to keep on a budget. We can
still do it—but only if you girls want it. You're the ones to
decide."

Without a minute's hesitation, Janice, Maxine, and
twelve-year-old Cathy agreed that they wanted Peggy to
continue—at least until 1968, when she would have another
chance at the Olympics.

Peggy enrolled that fall at Colorado College for three
courses and continued intensive practice at the Broadmoor.
The following winter she retained her U. S. title in Omaha
and then flew to Vienna to defend the World title.

"Skating in a bright rose costume, the slim, shy co-ed
from America's West outpointed all competitors and, for the
second straight year, won the title as world champion wom-
en's figure skater," reported one Austrian paper.

Another dubbed her "the fragile skater," and a third said
she was "America's shy Bambi."

It was true that her "ballet approach" to skating gave the
impression of fragile grace. It was also true that because she
is soft-spoken and somewhat reserved she did appear shy.
Peggy was beginning, though, to have fun with skating in a
way that was impossible in the early days of competition.

She told a magazine editor, "I've read in the newspapers
that I'm 'immensely shy.' Once I was described as 'cold, a
skater out of an icebox.' I wanted to shout 'No!' Actually I
was shy when I was younger and it *was* difficult for me to
project my feelings about skating to an audience. But I've
changed. Now I enjoy skating in front of people—the more
the merrier."

Several things had helped her overcome "inwardness."
One was the trick of looking up at the stands and pretend-
ing that they were filled not with rows of staring spectators

but with cabbages. Once she had that image fixed in her mind she could forget her nervousness and skate naturally. Another great help was a course in modern jazz dancing she took at college. Responding to the jazz beat "did lots to get me out of my shell," she said.

As 1967 drew to a close, training intensified. Three big challenges were ahead early in 1968: the U. S., the World, and the Winter Olympics. In January, Peggy successfully defended her national title for the fifth year.

"She has never been stronger or more graceful," reported a sportswriter. "She skated—floated actually—to an easy victory, a 109-pound wisp in an orange costume, and she made it look easy."

Her free-skating score from the U. S. Figure Skating Association judges was a breathtaking fraction below perfect: She received eight 5.9's and two 6's out of a possible ten 6's!

One month later she flew to Grenoble, France, with other American athletes to compete in the Winter Olympics. The ceremonies opened spectacularly: As 1291 athletes paraded, jet planes zoomed overhead wreathing the skies in colored smoke rings, fireworks flared, parachutists plummeted into Olympic rings, and 50,000 perfumed paper roses floated through the air into the stadium. It was a memorable opening to a week that proved to be almost unbearably high-pressure.

Peggy said later, "I kept thinking, 'It's not a matter of winning or losing for myself anymore. I'm representing my country. I've got to win.'"

At the Olympic ice rink, called "Stade de Glace," Peggy competed against thirty-one of the best skaters in the world. She took the lead in compulsory figures and then on Saturday presented a free-skating program that delighted the spectators: a blend of glides, spins, waltz jumps, double toe loops—all perfectly coordinated to the lilt of music.

On Saturday evening, when the judges announced the totals, Peggy Fleming of the United States, with 1970.5 points, was declared the winner—the only American to take a gold medal.

Standing on the three-tiered wooden steps to receive her medal and flanked by silver medalist Gabrielle Seyfert and bronze medalist Hana Maskova, she beamed and said, "No amount of money could ever give a person this feeling!"

One month later, in Switzerland, she took the World title for the third—and last—time. She was considering an offer to skate professionally, she told the press.

A reporter for *The New York Times* wrote: "At nineteen years of age, the delicate artistry and subtle movement of Peggy Fleming have brought her all the laurels that count —an Olympic championship, three world titles, and five American championships."

Her scores were in the official record books. She, like Tenley Albright and Carol Heiss, had made skating history.

Peggy packed her bags and with the other topflight amateurs went on a three-week exhibition tour. It included Iron Curtain countries like Yugoslavia, Romania, East Germany, and Russia. Russian skating fans applauded wildly and in Leningrad they pelted Peggy with flowers when she finished her free-skating program!

When it was finally over, she boarded a plane for home— with a stop-off in Washington. President Lyndon Johnson had invited her to the White House so he could congratulate her in person.

It had all started so simply: going to the Cleveland Arena with Janice that afternoon ten years before, lacing up skates and gliding onto the ice. What fun it was—stroking through the cool air.

"It's a wonderful sport," her father had said. *"It's a ladylike sport. I think you'll be good at it. . . ."*

"He Was Programmed to Take the Crunch . . . ."

Bill Moyers

The luncheon at the 40 Acres Club in Austin, Texas, that Friday in November, 1963, was an important one. The setting was elegant, the food and service were excellent. Talk flowed smoothly as officials of the Democratic party gathered to entertain their guest from Washington: Bill Moyers, the dynamic twenty-nine-year-old Texan who was Number Two man—deputy director—of the Peace Corps.

He was in his home state on a special assignment. President John Kennedy, Vice-President Lyndon Johnson, and their wives were touring the state—making short visits to the larger cities—to "mend political fences." Since Bill Moyers was one of the rare people respected by both Texas politicians and Kennedy supporters he had been asked to be a contact man for the trip.

Just the day before, on Thursday, November 21, the Presidential party had visited San Antonio, Houston, and Fort Worth and been welcomed warmly. The Friday schedule included an early appearance in Fort Worth, then Dallas in midday, and finally a gala reception at the governor's mansion in Austin that night, November 22.

There had been rumors that the President might be received with coolness—or even hostility—at some points in his visit and the Secret Service agents were guarding him closely. But in Houston Thursday afternoon, the streets had been lined with cheering crowds, and Friday morning in Fort Worth the President had joked with admirers who thronged the entrance to his hotel.

"Mrs. Kennedy is organizing herself," he explained with a broad smile when someone asked about the First Lady. "It takes longer, but, of course, she looks better than we do when she does it!"

Now, at noon, the President and his party would be in Dallas. Plans called for the limousines to proceed in a motorcade from Love Field. The open cars would travel along Lemmon Avenue and Turtle Creek Boulevard to Main Street and then out the Freeway, passing Dealey Plaza and the Texas School Book Depository.. . . .

Meanwhile in Austin the luncheon table buzzed with talk. At 12:42, a waiter stepped to the table: Mr. Moyers was wanted on the telephone. With a smile he excused himself and went to the phone booth. When he returned to the table a few minutes later his face was stony.

"The President has been shot and is believed dead," he told the men at the table. "The Governor has been shot and is critically wounded. The Vice-President is believed wounded."

The shocked group began peppering him with questions: How did it happen? Who fired the shots? Was it a conspiracy against the United States Government by an enemy nation?

Bill Moyers had no way to answer their questions. He had been told only the bare, tragic facts. As people began milling around the table, he sought out Frank Erwin, state chairman of the Democratic party, and asked if there was any way he could get to Dallas quickly. Lyndon Johnson had been his boss for years. If the Vice-President was in danger Bill wanted to offer his help.

Minutes later the two were racing to the Austin airport. Erwin chartered a plane to take Moyers to Dallas. It was while he was en route that the pilot picked up a radio bulletin:

"President John Kennedy has been pronounced dead."

While the little plane was boring through the sky toward Dallas, Secret Service agents were guarding the Vice-President and Mrs. Johnson in a cramped room at Parkland Memorial Hospital.

Just thirty minutes before, at 12:30 P.M., as the Presidential motorcade turned onto Elm Street and down the slope past the Texas School Book Depository, an assassin had aimed his rifle at the open limousine carrying President Kennedy, Governor John Connally, and their wives. Riding three cars behind, far out of range, were the Vice-President and Mrs. Johnson.

When the shots rang out and the President keeled over, Secret Service agent Rufus Youngblood vaulted into the Vice-President's car, slammed him to the floor, and crouched above him while the driver streaked seventy-seven blocks to Parkland Hospital.

Racing ahead of them was the limousine carrying John Kennedy—mortally wounded. Moments after it reached the hospital, the staff was mobilized in a frantic effort to save his life.

While doctors worked over him in Trauma Room One, agents ringed Lyndon Johnson and his wife and slipped them into another corridor. Agent Youngblood ordered a nurse to show them to a room that would be reasonably secure. A small booth (Number 13) in Minor Medicine was picked, and there the Vice-President and his wife waited behind drawn blinds and under heavy guard.

As minutes ticked away, one aide after another came to Booth 13 to confer with the agents or report hushed news from Trauma Room One. Someone located a vending machine and brought containers of coffee. The minutes ticked on.

The "Bagman," a walking courier who is always within instant call of the President of the United States and who carries a plain briefcase with emergency plans in case of enemy attack, had taken up his post immediately outside Trauma Room One.

At 12:50 a Kennedy aide reported that a priest had been sent for. "It looks pretty black," he told Lyndon Johnson.

Shortly after one o'clock, Emory Roberts, one of the agents, went to check on Kennedy's condition. At 1:13 P.M. he returned to Booth 13. Facing Johnson, he informed him, "The President is dead, sir."

The Bagman had left Trauma Room One and had now taken up his post outside Booth 13. With the last heartbeat of John Kennedy, the Presidency of the United States passed to the man who had been Vice-President.

On the advice of the Secret Service, Lyndon Johnson moved to get back to Washington as soon as possible. It was imperative for him to show the people of America—and the world —that although an assassin had cut down President Kennedy there would be a lawful, orderly transfer of government. The new head of state would carry on.

President Johnson and the First Lady were escorted from the hospital under heavy guard and driven in an unmarked car to Love Field. There, ringed by Secret Service men, they were bustled onto Air Force One, the Presidential jet.

Members of Kennedy's staff gravitated to another compartment. Here the coffin bearing the body of the slain President was placed and Mrs. Jacqueline Kennedy sat grieving.

"What's delaying us?" a Kennedy aide asked. "Why doesn't the pilot take off?"

"Mr. Johnson wants to take the oath of office here in Dallas," he was told. Judge Sarah Hughes of the U. S. District Court was hurrying to the airport to administer the Presidential oath, it was explained.

As the Presidential jet waited at Love Field, the small charter plane carrying Bill Moyers from Austin approached the airport and received clearance to land. It touched down almost within a wing's distance of Air Force One. Moyers could have been with Lyndon Johnson within minutes. He believed, however, that the Johnsons would still be at Parkland Hospital. Leaping into a state police car, he ordered the trooper to drive him there. While they were en route the police radio announced that the new President was, in fact, at Love Field. Still traveling at top speed, the trooper swung the car into a steep U-turn and streaked back to the airport.

There Moyers had no trouble mounting the front ramp of the Presidential jet. His tall, slim figure was known to several aides and he was passed along until he reached the final door.

"Sorry," said an agent, "I must stop you here." Three feet from him, on the other side of the closed door, was the man he had raced so frantically to see!

He scrawled a note on a slip of paper: "I'm here if you need me," and signed his name. The note was passed in and seconds later the door opened. The new President—his old boss—wanted him aboard. Bill Moyers slipped into the steamy compartment. Johnson glanced at him and nodded slightly but did not speak. Judge Sarah Hughes arrived soon afterward. As the photographer wrestled his equipment into place and began shooting pictures the oath of office was administered.

With his wife at one side and Mrs. Kennedy, who had come from her compartment, at the other, Lyndon Baines Johnson placed his left hand on a Bible, raised his right hand and repeated after Judge Hughes these words:

"I do solemnly swear that I will faithfully execute the office of President of the United States and will to the best of my ability preserve, protect and defend the Constitution of the United States."

He was now formally and publicly the 36th President. He embraced his wife and Mrs. Kennedy and then told his aides, "Let's get this plane back to Washington." Minutes later, with jets whining, Air Force One streaked into the sky. Mrs. Kennedy returned to her compartment, and President Johnson asked a few men to be seated with him. John Fitzgerald Kennedy, dead at forty-six, had left a huge void. Many of the men riding back to Washington with Johnson would be asked to help him fill that void. Soft-spoken Bill Moyers, at twenty-nine the youngest of the group, was one of them. At this particular moment, the new President had many reasons for including him.

Billy Moyers was born in Hugo, Oklahoma, on June 5, 1934, but his parents moved to Marshall, Texas, a town of 25,000 population in the eastern part of the state, when he was six months old. The Lone Star State was to be home for Billy and his seven-year-old brother, James, for many years.

America was just beginning to emerge from the depression which had racked it in the early 1930s. Jobs were scarce and John Henry Moyers worked long and hard at farming and other odd jobs to keep up with expenses at the small white house where the family lived. Both James and later Billy made good records in school. Studying was no problem for Billy. He was a wiry youngster, reed-thin but with enormous energy, and when he passed a street or store sign he could not resist the impulse to leap and swing on it —to see if the sign could "take it."

Not many could, his parents were informed.

To help family finances, Bill got a job after school and on Saturdays bagging groceries at the A & P in Marshall. In the fall of 1948, when he was fourteen, he entered Marshall High School. He was a lean boy with pale complexion and dark-rimmed glasses—quiet, reserved, impressing his teachers as verging on delicate health. But he soon surprised everyone: He plunged into activities at Marshall High at a rate that jolted brawnier classmates. He went out for the band, the cheerleading squad, the school paper, and dramatics—in his senior year he won the lead in a play about a minister, *One Foot in Heaven.* (Both the role and the play's title proved to be omens.)

It was a dizzying, nonstop round of activities; yet he managed to make a grade point average of 93.83.

"Billy Moyers worked like a house afire!" his adviser said later.

His regular assignment for *The Parrot,* the school newspaper, was sports reporting. He did such a good job that he rated another assignment, reporting school news for the Marshall *News-Messenger*. It was a paper his brother, James, had worked for and Bill found that Millard Cope, the publisher, was taking an interest in him and his plans for the future. One day Cope offered him a part-time job as a cub reporter. The part-time job grew and by the time he was fifteen he was covering regular news beats: city hall, police, political meetings. As a full-fledged reporter he rated a by-line. He asked the men in the composing room to set his name without the *y*. "Bill Moyers" sounded more grown-up, more dignified.

In June, 1952, he graduated from Marshall High School, fifth in a class of 143, and the following September went off to Denton, Texas, to enroll at North Texas State College. The pace he had set for himself in high school became standard. He took a job in the college news bureau and plunged into student politics and the Baptist Student Union. But he also managed his study time well: In his freshman and sophomore years he earned 24 A's and one B.

North Texas was lucky for Bill Moyers in many ways. His first week on campus he was assigned to an advanced English course. In the chair directly ahead sat a pretty co-ed with dark brown hair. When class was over she walked out without her books. The English professor asked Bill if he would be a good sport and "take Judith Davidson's books to her."

"Glad to!" he shot back. From that day on, Bill Moyers not only carried Judith's books regularly but became her regular date. By the time they were sophomores they were dating steadily enough to plan a wedding. The date was indefinite but would be at least two years in the future, after both had graduated from college.

His studies at college as a journalism major had whetted Bill's interest in American politics and that spring of his sophomore year he began to wonder about a career that would combine government and journalism.

He carefully composed a letter to Senator Johnson—

Lyndon Baines Johnson of his home state, the Senate Majority Leader. He asked about summer job opportunities in Mr.
Johnson's Washington office and gave as a reference the
name of Millard Cope, his old boss at the *News-Messenger*.

An answer came promptly: He had his job! Senator Johnson had checked with Cope, an old friend, and received
such a glowing report on the energetic young reporter that
he was hiring him, sight unseen.

Bill announced the news proudly to Judith and to his parents. Washington! A job in the Senate Office Building! Bill
Moyers from Marshall, Texas, would have a chance to work
at the nerve center of American politics.

He reported for work one day in June, 1954, and was
given his first assignment: labeling addresses on 100,000
copies of Senator Johnson's newsletter. His equipment: an
ancient foot-pedal-operated machine that creaked alarm-
ingly every time an envelope was fed into it. It was not
quite what the ambitious young man from Texas had expected.

Alone with the metal monster and what seemed a mountain of mail, Bill learned, little by little, its eccentricities and
turned out the newsletters in good time. The office staff was
impressed. He was given a chance to answer routine letters
from Texas voters and then was promoted to handling some
of the Senator's personal correspondence.

Bill was in close contact with the tall, high-domed, drawl-
ing lawmaker frequently every week. Yet there were times
when he doubted that his boss was aware of his existence.

Johnson himself had first come to Washington twenty
years before as secretary to a congressman. But he was Senate Majority Leader now; his lines of communication ran to
people in the highest echelons of power and he had so many
responsibilities to discharge. . . . It was foolish to think he
could pay much attention to a twenty-year-old office assistant!

As the steamy Washington summer dragged to an end
Bill felt his frustration growing. Government and politics

fascinated him. But the system was so huge, so complicated, it overwhelmed him.

"Washington frustrated me," was the way he put it. "It wasn't just that I was young and parochial. I just didn't see how one person—particularly someone of my ilk—could shape much that was important in this town. . . . I was afraid I could never make much of a mark in public affairs."

Should he play it safe and stay with journalism, the field that had brought him income since he was fifteen years old? He was sure he could make a success in some branch of journalism. Yet he felt a powerful drive to serve, to lift, to make some contribution to humanity. He had hoped to find in public affairs an outlet for this drive. But after a long summer in Washington he knew he would have to choose again. Should he pour his energies and ambition into teaching? Perhaps.

Or the ministry?

His parents had joined the Baptist church in Marshall when Bill was twelve years old, and little by little his commitment to religion had grown deeper during his high-school and college years.

As his summer in Washington drew to an end, he decided that his ambition to serve could be satisfied best in the ministry. The road ahead was studded with formidable hurdles, though. Bill and Judith had two years to complete at North Texas before their marriage. When they graduated in 1956 Bill would enter the seminary for three years and then take a church. It would be five years before they could settle down to a life of stability and relief from high pressure.

Five years of scrimping for tuition, living on the tightest budget for food, clothes, a tiny apartment. But it would be worth it . . . if he could prepare himself for a life of service, Bill knew.

Johnson, who rarely took time to talk with Bill, asked him one day at the end of the summer if he was satisfied with North Texas. Bill answered that he and his fiancée both loved it and were avidly involved in activities on the Denton campus.

"Why not consider the U. of Texas at Austin?" the Senator asked. He pointed out that Bill could take a variety of courses there—many that Denton did not offer. Johnson himself had gone to a small teachers' college in the state, he told Bill, and had come to value the lively, more sophisticated campus at Austin

Equally important, he added, there was a part-time job open as assistant news editor at KTBC in Austin, the radio-TV station owned by Mrs. Johnson. The job was Bill's if he wanted it. The salary, $300 a month, would mean that Bill and Judith could get married at the start of their junior year.

Senator Johnson liked the spirit, the spunk of his summer aide. Things in the younger man's background paralleled elements in his own. Both had their roots in the Southwest and in small-town America. Both respected education for opening doors to the good life. (They knew too many dropouts who had to scrounge for jobs as dishwashers and day laborers!) Both had tireless energy that could drive one to a goal with buzz-saw speed.

Twenty years before, Lyndon Johnson, then an obscure young Texan, had been encouraged by President Franklin D. Roosevelt. Roosevelt, he said later, ". . . was like a daddy to me."

Now the most powerful man in the U. S. Senate, Johnson was, in turn, helping another young Texan. For Bill Moyers, the summer that had started so humbly with the foot-pedal addresser and sacks of mail was ending handsomely.

Bill and Judith enrolled at Texas U. in Austin the following September and were married at Christmas vacation. Home was a $40-a-month apartment just off campus. As it turned out, though, they had little time to spend as homebodies. Bill's job as assistant news editor at KTBC was on a part-time basis. He batted out radio news at such a furious clip, however, that senior writers taught him to write weather reports, commercials, and almost everything else broadcast daily.

With each new job he learned, his work hours escalated. The "part-time" assignment grew to a fifty-hour workweek! (Today the station has eight employees doing the work that he turned out alone while he was finishing college.)

The pace he set for himself approached perpetual motion. The tall transfer student from North Texas State College began logging sixteen- and seventeen-hour workdays that would have left an Olympic wrestler crying for mercy. He was up at 4:30 and off to KTBC to work from 5 until 8 A.M. He raced back home to have breakfast with his bride. ("It was usually the only meal we had together," says Judith.) Then the newlyweds were off to class: Judith to home economics (her major) or chemistry (her minor); Bill to journalism classes or to study Greek, which he knew would be required in seminary.

"We met on campus and had lunch together—sometimes," says his wife. "But not often. Most days I'd see him at breakfast and again at eight or nine at night—whenever he finished at the station."

His class schedule had been arranged so that he could shuttle back and forth between KTBC and his classrooms. At almost any time between 5 A.M. and 9 P.M. when Bill was not in class he was writing radio news or roaming the streets of Austin in a KTBC mobile unit on the track of a news story. Puzzled classmates were sure he studied—but when?

"He studied on the run," says his wife with a wry smile.

His weight hovered at the 130-pound mark, far too low for his six-foot frame, and he was troubled with weak eyesight; but he was determined to do justice to both college and the job. He also had taken on another responsibility: serving two tiny country churches on alternate Sunday mornings as a Baptist lay preacher.

The Southwest had been gripped by severe drought for

BILL MOYERS | 175

years, and the farm families who came to hear the young preacher bore the marks of worry and deprivation in their weather-beaten faces. They came to the wind-scorched church on Sunday mornings hungry for a worship service that would lift and sustain their spirits. And they found it in the straightforward sermons that the young college student brought them.

Moyers had learned years before as a newspaper cub to tell a story in forceful, simple language. Now he was applying that lesson to his sermons. The response was immediate.

"He doesn't sound preachy," the farmers often told Judith after a service. In the two years that he served this region blighted by drought and studded with ghost towns, the farmers and their families came to look on the young couple with deep affection. His wife recalls them as "wonderful people—just wonderful." Preaching to them made such an impression on Bill that he later said the peaceful Shiloh church graveyard would be a perfect place to be laid to rest.

It was known at KTBC that Bill was headed for the ministry—some of the staff called him "Bishop." Far from being solemn and straight-faced, though, this "Bishop" turned out to be a prankster. He and a co-worker invented a gag "charity drive" and set out small "collection" cans around the station with the initials: S.U.T.A.H. or, as Bill explained with a grin: "Send Us to Alluring Hawaii!"

When a radio announcer squirted him with a water pistol he retaliated by setting off a firecracker in the studio when the announcer was on the air. It jarred the man's nerves so badly that he chased Bill out of the building and down the street, leaving KTBC listeners with "dead air" for five minutes.

In the spring of his senior year, Bill began to look ahead to entering the seminary. His record was impressive: His grade average was 2.77 out of a possible 3.0 and he won the Cabot Award for the senior journalism student with the highest four-year scholastic record. He would have no problem being accepted as a seminary student—but which school should he choose?

Talking it over one day with his old friend Millard Cope, publisher of the *News-Messenger,* he reviewed some of the schools that attracted him.

"Why not take a break—take a year off?" Cope suggested. "Leave the States and study overseas for a year. You'll have new perspective when you come back."

The Rotary Club gave an international fellowship for study overseas, Cope said, and it would mean $3000 for a year of study—and travel.

Bill applied and was accepted with the understanding that the $3000 would be used only for *his* studies and living expenses—not his wife's. She would have to find a job and be self-supporting so that Bill could be a full-time student— for the first time since grade school.

In late summer they left Texas for the University of Edinburgh in Scotland. For the next year Bill studied the relationship of church and state while Judith taught "domestic science" to girls in a sadly antiquated Scottish school where most girls were headed for a life of drudgery in the local cotton mills. She taught such things as building a wood fire in a stove and how to do the family laundry by boiling clothes.

"It was the kind of course taught in the States thirty or forty years ago," she says. "I learned new respect for American high-school education that year in Scotland!"

When Bill's courses at the university were finished he and Judith were able to enjoy the "travel" privileges of the Rotary grant. They toured Europe by car for three months, sleeping in hostels when they could, to save money, and hitchhiking when their car broke down.

Bill enrolled at Southwestern Baptist Theological Seminary in Fort Worth that September, 1957. His training in journalism again proved a help—he got a job as director of information for the seminary and held it for two years until graduation.

A baby son—William Cope—was born to Bill and Judith Moyers in May, 1959. Graduation was scheduled for December, and he had two job offers to consider: a call to a church in Hawkins, Texas, and a teaching post as instructor in ethics at Baylor U.

Somehow neither one seemed right. Five years before, when Bill had first felt the need to do something idealistic, something with deep meaning, he was sure it could be expressed best in the ministry. All his energies—and Judith's —had been channeled to that end. Yet now, just weeks before graduation, nagging doubts plagued him. His drive to lift—to serve—was as strong as ever. Many young ministers would have satisfied it either in the pulpit or in the classroom. Some impulse told Bill, though, that the way to fulfill his ideals was by taking another road. What road? He wasn't sure. . . .

With graduation only weeks away, he finally accepted the post at Baylor. He would move Judith, himself, and the baby to the campus after Christmas and teach his first courses during the spring semester while beginning work for his doctorate.

His parents, who had taken great pride in Bill's scholastic records—and especially in his ordination—were tremendously pleased that he was going to teach at a Baptist college.

All in all, it was the wise, the prudent choice for him to make. The career he could make for himself and his family on a university campus would be solid and satisfying. He and Judith could settle down after all the years of hard work and the hectic pace and make a quiet life for themselves.

Then one day in November the telephone rang.

It was Senator Johnson, Bill's old boss, calling to ask if he would consider a short assignment. Several influential men had persuaded Johnson to try for the 1960 Presidential nomination on the Democratic ticket. Sen. John Kennedy of Massachusetts was a strong contender and Adlai Stevenson, the 1956 candidate, would also be in the running. If Johnson was to make a strong showing he would have to have a team of hardworking people handling speeches, travel arrangements, and press conferences. Would Bill Moyers join that team on a temporary basis—just until the Democrats picked their man in July?

Bill turned it over in his mind and then agreed. He would have to ask Baylor to give him a postponement until the fall semester, but he was sure it would work out all right.

He felt good about going back to political life for this short assignment. The pace would be hard-driving and hectic in the months leading up to the convention. But afterward he would be back in Texas, leading the life of a college teacher.

Senator Johnson hadn't mentioned salary—and Moyers hadn't asked. But he wasn't worried—about money or taking this job. Somehow it felt right. And over the years he had learned to trust this feeling.

Bill, Judith, and the baby moved to Washington to the apartment of a friend and Bill plunged into the business of planning strategy for the Democratic convention. The demands on him ranged from simple to complex: He was organizer for appointments, press statements, and correspondence.

The young secretaries in the Senator's office thought it quite a novelty to have an ordained minister working waist-deep in a rough, tough political fracas. They soon had to admit, though, that the new young aide had a genius for organizing office routines and could work under terrific pressure without snarling or snapping.

Early in July the Johnson forces flew to Los Angeles. The Biltmore Hotel was headquarters for both Johnson and Kennedy, and as the convention opened, staff members began working around the clock. Would the Senator from Texas— or from Massachusetts—take first place on the ticket? The work of lining up delegate strength for the big push on the convention floor called for all-out effort. Hour after blistering hour, as telephones jangled and visitors streamed through the Johnson suite, Bill Moyers kept details clicking into place and conversations flowing smoothly—especially between the Johnson suite and Room 8314, where Robert Kennedy was planning strategy for his brother.

These were the peak crisis hours when staff people could not take time to sleep normally. When they were bone-tired and glassy-eyed they showered, sipped soup, or stretched out for a quick nap. (Bill took his on a cot that was put up in an outsize closet!)

On Wednesday night, July 14, when balloting began at the Los Angeles Sports Arena, John Fitzgerald Kennedy was nominated as candidate for President on the Democratic ticket. A total of 761 votes was required to win the nomination: The young Senator from Massachusetts drew 806. The tally for Senator Johnson of Texas was 409.

Who would be the choice for Vice-President? Newspaper and TV reporters announced confidently that Sen. Stuart Symington of Missouri was favored. There was a slim possibility that John Kennedy might spring a surprise, though.

On Thursday morning a message from Room 8314 came to the Johnson suite: Senator Kennedy was calling to say he would be down shortly. At 10 A.M. he arrived and asked Lyndon Johnson to be his running mate on the Democratic ticket. The handsome young New Englander, who had just passed his forty-third birthday, sat on a couch across from the veteran Texan and told him forthrightly that he felt a Kennedy-Johnson ticket would appeal to all sections of the country.

Both men understood the unspoken truth behind this statement. Kennedy was a Roman Catholic and a liberal—facts that conservative Southern voters would worry about. Johnson would "balance" the ticket.

Johnson accepted and promised to work hard for their victory in November.

For Moyers the prospect of teaching that September was fading fast.

From July 15 until the election of Kennedy and Johnson in November, Moyers remained in the front ranks of the Johnson staff coordinating travel schedules, working with the press, and serving as majordomo on the candidate's personal plane. Setting up travel arrangements for the speeches Johnson was making on the campaign trail took hours every day.

In November, when the Kennedy-Johnson ticket was elected by a narrow margin, Moyers began to take stock of his prospects for a future in Washington. He had decided to stay in the capital—but not in the comfortable job of aide to the Vice-President. He had been looking for a post that would offer human service. Now he was sure he had found it in an organization called the Peace Corps.

In launching the corps, President Kennedy had said, "I want to demonstrate to Mr. Khrushchev and others that a new generation of Americans has taken over this country . . . young Americans who will serve the cause of freedom as servants of peace around the world, working for freedom as the Communists work for their system."

The more Bill learned about the project the more he wanted to be part of it. "The Peace Corps idea gnawed at me," is the way he put it.

Johnson was reluctant to let him go at first. But Bill was quietly determined. During his years at the seminary he had come across a statement by Thomas Jefferson: "The care of human life and happiness . . . is the first and only legitimate object of good government." It capsuled his own feelings about public service—and the Peace Corps would be the best place to put them into practice.

Sargent Shriver had just been appointed director of the corps. A friend of Johnson's wrote to Shriver recommending Moyers. He ended his letter this way:

"If I were a young man, I think I would be content at the age of twenty-six to be the top assistant of the Vice-President. But this boy Moyers is willing to give this up, without a backward look, so he can 'do good.' The world is full—and the Peace Corps will be—of people who want to 'do good' and have not the slightest idea how. This young man knows how. He is that curious and very rare blend of idealist-operator."

The letter convinced Shriver. Moyers was named one of five associate directors of the Peace Corps in its most critical —and most exciting—period. How would young men and women be recruited and trained? Who would determine which countries should get Peace Corps programs? How long should the assignments for corpsmen be—one year, two years? What about legislation—and funds? All had to be answered in this formative early period.

President Kennedy had spoken of "young Americans who will serve the cause of freedom as servants of peace around the world." It was a beautiful, bold ideal, but it could be torpedoed by critics in Congress. Many congressmen were skeptical: Why should the United States Government send "kids" and middle-aged farmers to Ecuador and Ethiopia to live in village huts and work with their hands?

Convincing them that the Peace Corps was not only idealistic but would work to the long-range advantage of the United States was Moyers's assignment. Using the contacts he had developed as Johnson's aide, he set up appointments with more than 500 members of Congress so that he and Sargent Shriver could explain to each of them what the corps hoped to achieve if it had the necessary support—and funds—from Congress.

The soft-spoken courtesy and conviction shown by Moyers and Shriver in these face-to-face meetings with skeptics on Capitol Hill began to take effect. Several admitted that this Peace Corps idea might be worth a trial, after all.

Legislation which Moyers supervised in its draft stages was sent to Congress and passed. By the end of 1961 recruits were in training camps and early in 1962 the first 500 corpsmen were flying off to assignments.

The project so infuriated the Communists that they labeled Shriver "a bloodthirsty Chicago butcher and sausage-maker" and called the Peace Corps "a nest of spies." When the first young Americans began arriving in villages in Africa and the Middle East to teach farming methods and baby-health routines, however, it was plain—even to mistrustful local government members—that they had come to teach and to serve. A very strange "nest of spies"!

For Bill Moyers, his work with the Peace Corps was a dream assignment: It was all the things he had worked toward—creative, challenging, humanitarian. As associate director in charge of public affairs he had to be fast-thinking and resourceful. The recruitment drive depended on ads in newspapers and magazines, bus cards, and television "spots," and his instinct for picking them was sure. Sargent Shriver said, "Bill would take a stack of ad slogans and tick them off: 'This one, not that. This one, not that.' "

Gradually the bugs in the program were being eliminated and gradually, too, skeptics were accepting the fact that Americans could go off to remote parts of the world and help other human beings on a person-to-person basis. ". . . working for freedom as the Communists work for their system," as President Kennedy had said.

The 500 first authorized by Congress grew to 5000 by March, 1963, and the next year to 10,000—working in forty-six countries by invitation.

"The corps has been able," said Moyers, "to take an idealistic dream and develop it into an effective program." He added that his pride in being part of it was boundless. "Few things in life can be as satisfying."

In January, 1963, at the age of twenty-eight, he was named deputy director of the Peace Corps—the Number 2 job and one that several of the brightest young men in Washington had competed for. It was a Presidential appointment that required Senate confirmation. Some senators grumbled about his age. "How old are you?" barked one of them as Bill Moyers appeared before them.

"I'm twenty-eight—and a half," he answered smoothly.

Others remarked that his salary for the new job was "exorbitant." They did not know that he had just received a job offer—outside of government—of $30,000 a year and had turned it down to stay with the Peace Corps for $19,500.

As deputy director he began working an exhausting schedule, and an ulcer was one result. But there were great compensations, not only in his job but in his personal life. In August, 1962, a baby daughter, Suzanne, had been born to Bill and Judith Moyers, and life in Washington was stable and happy as 1963 drew to an end.

One day in November a call came from Kenneth O'Donnell of the White House staff. President Kennedy and Vice-President Johnson planned to tour the state of Texas. Would Bill Moyers take a short trip to his home state and pave the way for the President's visit?

He left the following week and on Friday, November 22, was in Austin. He was a guest at lunch at the 40 Acres Club and talk around the table was about the way Texans were receiving the President's visit. The stops at San Antonio and Houston the day before had been huge successes. Dallas was to be visited that afternoon.

Plans called for the Presidential plane, Air Force One, to land at Love Field in Dallas. The President and the other dignitaries (Vice-President Johnson, Governor Connally, and their wives) would then take their places in limousines —with the tops down—and drive through the streets of Dallas.

Riding in open cars was risky. The Secret Service guarding the President had warned against it. But Kennedy believed that there should be no barrier between himself and the people. A President should show himself and get close to them.

Would Dallas receive him with as much warmth as did Houston and San Antonio and Fort Worth? The men lunching with Bill Moyers in Austin that Friday noon were optimistic. Texans were, after all, known around the world for their warmth and cordiality to visitors.

When the parade and luncheon in Dallas were over that afternoon President Kennedy and Vice-President Johnson were to return to Air Force One and fly here to Austin, the state capital, to be welcomed by the men Bill Moyers was lunching with.

A waiter stepped to the table. "Mr. Moyers? There's a call for you from Dallas."

He went to the telephone. The message was terse, tragic: President Kennedy had been shot by a sniper and was dying or dead. Governor Connally, riding in the same car, had been wounded. There were unconfirmed reports that Vice-President Johnson had been injured also. The city of Dallas was in the grip of shock, and wild rumors were spreading unchecked.

When Bill Moyers brought the news back to the luncheon group, he was swamped with questions: Was it the work of an individual? Had he been caught? Could it be part of a global conspiracy? Were enemies of America plotting to kill all high members of the government and paralyze the nation so they could seize control?

Moyers could not answer their urgent questions. He told them only the bare facts that had been relayed to him. At this point he was sure of only one thing: If his old boss, Lyndon Johnson, was wounded or in danger Bill should go to him.

It was shortly after this that Frank Erwin agreed to help. He could charter a plane at the Austin airport that would take Moyers to Dallas. . . .

The Kennedy assassination had, in fact, been the deed of an individual, not part of a global conspiracy. But at the moment John Kennedy was pronounced dead and Lyndon Johnson became his successor the Secret Service did not know this. Their urgent duty was to guard the new President and get him safely out of Dallas and back to Washington.

So it was that Mr. Johnson and his wife were bustled out of Parkland Hospital and driven—crouching to keep their heads below window level—to the safety of the Presidential jet at Love Field.

Here Bill Moyers eventually joined him and witnessed the historic swearing-in of Lyndon Baines Johnson as thirty-sixth President of the United States.

A gigantic task lay ahead of the new President. John Fitzgerald Kennedy, killed by an assassin at forty-six, was leaving a tremendous void. He was a handsome, witty man whose image for millions of Americans—and for people around the world—was one of vigor and confidence.

He had been in the White House less than three years, yet he had signed a nuclear test ban treaty with Russia. He had achieved the strongest civil-rights bill in history. And he had made Khrushchev back down in the Cuban missile crisis. Now he was dead, and the American people were shocked—and fearful.

Who was this man Johnson? Would he stand up to America's enemies as coolly and resolutely as John Kennedy had? Would he be a true President for all Americans . . . the old and the young, the powerful and the weak? Would he have secret loyalties—or hatreds? He had been plunged into power so quickly that he might well fumble and allow evil men to pressure him into doing the wrong thing.

America was waiting to see how this man from Texas would handle the tremendous power that was now his. If his hand on the controls was sure and steady, if he was honorable and unbiased, America could recover from its shock and carry on. The question in the minds of billions of people around the world was, "What will happen now?"

Lyndon Baines Johnson had to give the right answer.

Air Force One landed at Andrews Air Force Base outside Washington at 6:05 P.M. The body of the murdered President was lifted down gently, respectfully and placed in a Navy ambulance. President and Mrs. Johnson then left the jet and walked into the glare of lights to face cameras and microphones.

"This is a sad time for all people," said Johnson in a voice that was tightly controlled. "We have suffered a loss that cannot be weighed. For me it is a deep personal tragedy. I know the world shares the sorrow that Mrs. Kennedy and her family bear. I will do my best. That is all I can do. I ask for your help—and God's."

When he finally reached home that night, after a stop at his old office in the Executive Office Building, he was received by a few close friends. With Johnson on his first night as President were men he could trust implicitly to hear his thoughts and plans; and three of them—Jack Valenti, Horace Busby, and Bill Moyers—were asked to spend the night.

Shortly after twelve the President said good-night. But his mind was too full of the day's happenings; he couldn't sleep. He called the three guests to his room and began to talk about the things that must be done that day. What matters had to be done immediately? Which world leaders—coming for the Kennedy funeral that weekend—should he confer with?

Until 3 A.M. Moyers and two other men sat planning with the President. There were two telephone calls to be made that could not wait even until morning: one to the Central Intelligence Agency, the other to Robert McNamara, Secretary of Defense. The television set in the President's bedroom was on and he watched it intently from time to time for news: Several members of the Kennedy cabinet had been flying to Japan on a mission and had turned back in mid-Pacific.

When Johnson finally said good-night he had asked these three—Valenti, Busby, and Moyers—to stay with him, to be members of his staff. It was understood that Bill Moyers's assignment would be a loan from the Peace Corps. He would work at the White House with his old boss until he had a firm grasp of his duties as President. Then Moyers would go back to the work that was giving him so much pride and satisfaction. For the immediate present, though, he was putting this dream job out of his mind so he could concentrate on helping his boss through the first tumultuous days of taking control of the United States.

Serving as schedule planner, assistant, and regulator of the flow of visitors' traffic into and out of the President's office, Moyers worked at Johnson's side for hectic hours on end. The feverish activity he had endured at the 1960 Los Angeles convention seemed only a mild warm-up for this forked-lightning period following the Kennedy assassination.

Always a hard worker, Lyndon Johnson now drove himself relentlessly. The men he had picked to work on his staff had to be on call at any hour of the day or night. Moyers sat at a desk directly outside the President's office in these early days and many of the secret communiqués affecting the safety of the United States flowed through him. Hour by hour he dealt with dispatches from Vietnam, the Congo, the Middle East. He met many of the visitors who came to talk with President Johnson. The morning after the Kennedy funeral, the Chancellor of Germany, the Prime Minister of Great Britain, and the Deputy Premier of the U.S.S.R. called to have individual conferences with the new President.

Later that week there were appointments with Americans who knew the problems that this country faced; businessmen, labor leaders, editors streamed by Moyers's desk.

At the Peace Corps, he had kept his ulcer under control by sipping strawberry milkshakes. The White House did not have soda-fountain facilities, so he switched to ice cream—a pint a day.

Each day he became more and more responsible for handling affairs for President Johnson. "He's my vice-president in charge of anything," Johnson told a reporter.

Yet he refused to join the Presidential payroll. He was still officially on leave from the Peace Corps. Even his old office was intact and waiting for him.

"I'm just here helping a friend," he said. "When the emergency is over I'll drift away and never be heard of again!"

Weeks lengthened into months. By mid-1964 Johnson and his aide reached a meeting of minds about the future: The election of 1964 faced the President. If Moyers would stay on during the Democratic convention in Atlantic City and through the November election, he could go back to the Peace Corps. Equally important, he would be in line to take over as director of the corps: Sargent Shriver had been named director of the War on Poverty and would be leaving the Number 1 job.

Director of the Peace Corps! Bill Moyers would go back to the work he loved, moving into the directorship. He was elated.

In November, 1964, Lyndon Johnson was elected to a full term as President by defeating the Republican candidate, Barry Goldwater. By then Moyers had taken on so many duties, had coordinated, scheduled, and arranged so many matters and been troubleshooter in so many crises that he had been named Johnson's chief of staff.

His dream of returning to the Peace Corps was fading. The longer he stayed at the White House, at the nerve center of power, the more he realized the contribution he could make. He had moved to a spacious office in the west wing of the White House and there he handled a staggering variety of top-level problems.

One writer described it this way: "On a given day Bill Moyers may confer in depth with as many as three Cabinet officers on such divergent and complex subjects as water pollution, juvenile delinquency, and fair labor standards legislation. Between conferences he may brief a group of visiting editors on the aims of the Great Society, settle a jurisdictional dispute between two government departments and answer complaints from half a dozen members of Congress. . . . He attends all meetings of both the Cabinet and the National Security Council and, since 1965, has regularly pulled duty on overseas crises."

When *Time* did a front-cover profile on him they wrote,

"Moyers has access to virtually every secret document in the National Archives, is a regular at the exclusive Tuesday luncheons with Johnson and his Big Three on foreign affairs: Secretary of State Dean Rusk, Defense Secretary Robert McNamara, and Special Assistant McGeorge Bundy."

If working at the White House was an exhausting, nerve-jolting business, it was also exciting and satisfying.

"By late '65 when the Administration's legislative program began to move through Congress I began to see how a man who worked for the President can help shape things," Moyers told a reporter. "All the things I had been thinking about for months were becoming law. That was a turning point. My hope of returning to the Peace Corps gave way to the realization that the real power to get things done was right here—in the White House. Very few men have the opportunity to serve the President of the United States."

Shortly before Johnson took anesthesia for his gallbladder operation, Moyers was delegated to decide if—or when—in an emergency, Vice-President Hubert Humphrey should take over the powers of the Presidency. Lyndon Johnson was satisfied that the assistant he sometimes affectionately called "my preacher" would make the right decision.

The relationship between the two Texans seemed, at times, almost that of father and son. Yet this "father" could be difficult. When he was under pressure he barked at members of his staff and snarled at secretaries.

"You probably have to be a yes-man to get along with Johnson," a news editor said to Moyers one day.

On the contrary, he told the man, yessing Lyndon Johnson was a sure way to "get his back up." "The times I've heard him really light into the staff were times when he thought we were shaving our judgment," he said.

Members of Johnson's staff were expected not only to go to bat for their ideas but to stand up under awesome pressure. Jack Valenti, Douglass Cater, Richard Goodwin, and others all possessed this ability but probably none to the same high degree that Bill Moyers did. This was especially true during the time when he served as press secretary in addition to all his other jobs. His poise under a barrage of questions impressed even hard-boiled reporters.

"He lights up one of his pencil-thin cigars and fields any hot question we fire at him," said one.

Another put it this way: "When the pressure's on—the Dominican Republic crisis, for instance—you know Moyers won't push the panic button. He's programmed to take the crunch."

A third child, John, had been born to Bill and Judith Moyers in 1964. Although the White House put enormous demands on his time, he was determined not to be an "absentee father." He often worked late and couldn't see Cope, Suzanne, and the baby before they went to bed. The way to solve the problem, he found, was to get up at 6:15 for an early family breakfast and then have an hour's romp with them before a chauffeur-driven limousine from the White House called at their home in McLean, Virginia, to take him to work.

"People who saw him only on business usually thought of him as serious," says Judith, "but he's full of fun. When he's with the children it comes out—he plays hide-and-seek with them and romps and clowns. And they love it!"

Bill Moyers's assignment for Lyndon Johnson, which began so dramatically in Dallas on that tragic Friday, November 22, 1963, came to a quiet end. One day in late summer, 1966, Moyers telephoned a message to Capt. Harry F. Guggenheim, owner and editor-in-chief of *Newsday*, a newspaper in Garden City, L. I. Guggenheim had dealt with the White House many times, and the energetic young Texan who worked at such a furious pace had long impressed him.

Talking with Moyers that day on a routine matter, Guggenheim said on the spur of the moment, "Bill, everybody leaves the government sooner or later. When you're ready to go, how about coming to *Newsday?*"

The offer was a handsome one. He would become publisher—at age thirty-two—of a daily newspaper with a hefty circulation of more than 500,000, the largest suburban paper in the country. In a post like this he could apply the knowledge of American government and world affairs acquired in many jobs in Washington. And in a very real sense, he could be of service to the individual.

To Bill Moyers, city-hall reporter for the Marshall, Texas, *News-Messenger* when he was a fifteen-year-old high-school student, the offer was irresistible. He submitted his resignation to President Johnson in late fall, asking that it take effect in February, 1967.

Moyers had worked for Lyndon Johnson three times and in jobs that ranged from mail clerk to adviser on top-level problems. His loyalty to this Texan who drove himself and his staff relentlessly was deep-rooted and complete. Yet he could look at the Chief with objectivity and a wry sense of humor. Once a secretary with a zeal for history started reminding the staff to save all of Mr. Johnson's papers and "other personal effects" for the archives. A few days later, a lumpy envelope—specked with grease—was delivered to her desk.

"What is this?" she asked, peering inside.

Moyers explained with a slight smile that he was making a contribution to her collection: chicken bones from the President's lunch!

On a wintry day in January, 1967, shortly before Moyers left Washington, visitors to his handsome office found him completing the last assignments for Lyndon Johnson. Spacious windows, draped from floor to ceiling, looked out on the front lawn. Behind a semicircular desk sat the soft-spoken man who was credited with generating more far-reaching projects than any other single member of the President's staff.

During his years in Washington many people had written accusing him of "deserting" the ministry for the tough, cynical world of politics. Men who had worked with him in the tempestuous years after Kennedy's death could have answered in his defense. It was true that Bill Moyers—like the minister in his high-school play—had had only "one foot in heaven." But he had made sure the other was firmly planted on Capitol Hill, where he could influence legislation for millions of poor and uneducated Americans.

As he had told a reporter for *The New York Times*, "I cringe at all this publicity. That's not where the satisfaction comes. News clippings always have a way of fading, but no one can ever take away the fact that the Higher Education Act and the Elementary Education Act bear something of my mark—even if only a tiny toeprint."

"You Just Get Out on That Stage and Sing!"

Shirley Verrett

She swung the car onto a curving, palm-draped street and stopped in front of a stucco house. On the lawn a metal "For Sale" sign glinted in the sun.

"This is the place," she said, turning to the couple in the back seat. "Number 43. We just got the listing last week. The owner is being transferred out of town. It has two bedrooms and a bath downstairs——"

"I don't like this neighborhood!" snapped the man. "What kind of people live on this block?"

The young saleswoman turned a cool gaze on him. "Very nice people," she said quietly. "*Very* nice."

"Well, I'm not sure about this neighborhood," grunted the man. "Somebody was telling me that this area is going downhill. They might rezone it 'Commercial.'"

"Not here," she answered. "This is strictly residential. Besides, I wouldn't show you a house you'd be unhappy with."

The man snorted. "Maybe *you* wouldn't—but plenty of real-estate people in Los Angeles would say anything to make a fast deal!"

"Why don't we call it a day?" his wife said hastily. "We've looked at a lot of houses. I'm sure Miss Verrett is tired. Maybe she can call us if she gets some other listings."

Without a word, she headed the car back to the office. The black leather folder beside her on the front seat contained at least a dozen cards listing homes that might be possibilities. But Shirley Verrett was not going to mention them to these people—today or ever.

The wife was pleasant enough. But her husband, a big, burly man, was impossible to please. They had seen six houses that day, and he had sneered at all six. He was a faultfinding old crab. Too bad he couldn't buy a hermit's hut in the Sierra Nevada Mountains!

Shirley Verrett was not in the habit of thinking harshly of people. She loved most people—truly loved them. During her high-school and junior-college years she had been known for being warm and friendly.

"When Shirley smiles, the sun comes up over the Grand Canyon!" a friend once said about her.

But lately she had felt like snarling, not smiling. Something was wrong. It was almost as if her whole inner self had split and warped.

She knew the reason: Selling real estate was not what she wanted to do at all. She wanted to sing professionally on the concert stage and maybe in opera. And here she was driving prospects around Los Angeles showing houses for sale!

She had forced herself to do it because her family had convinced her it was a good, sensible, *practical* way to earn a living . . . very little risk involved . . . very little chance to fail. . . .

But very little satisfaction for someone with musical talent! Shirley wanted to sing so much it was getting to be an ache. Maybe the time to do something about it was now. . . .

A career in music? Shirley's father had always been doggedly opposed to it. One of God's great gifts to His creatures on earth was music, he believed. And it behooves His creatures to use that gift to glorify Him. One of the best ways to do it, he declared, was singing in church, especially his own Seventh-Day Adventist church.

Years before, when Shirley was a little girl in New Orleans, she could remember going to church with her mother, sister, and four brothers and watching Leon Verrett sing with the choir. When they lifted their voices in one of the old hymns, the walls rang. Hope—and hurt—was in that choir music.

There was music at home too. Shirley's brothers were always taking turns at the piano, picking out tunes. If they brought home a friend who played drums or a horn there was an "instant orchestra" in the living room.

Leon and his wife, Elvira, loved those sessions—so long as they didn't get too loud or too jazzy. They were loving parents but also strict. They wanted all their children to grow up religiously.

Shirley could pick out tunes on the family piano but not so well as her brothers. Her talent was singing. She had a rich, warm voice that her father recognized as having a rare quality.

"Shirley, let me hear you do 'Abide With Me,' " he would say.

As she sang the old hymn he listened intently.

"Very nice, honey. Now let's try it again, and this time I want to hear the words. Don't slur them. And don't let your voice fade away at the end."

When she sang it finally to his satisfaction he gave her a hug. All this coaching at home probably meant that some day soon she would be singing in the choir. What a thrill that would be, singing with all the other people!

But her father kept putting her off. "When you're good enough to sing a *solo* you'll sing in church," he told her.

A solo? Lots of *grown* people did not have that chance very often.

"Wouldn't it be all right if I sang with them for practice?" she asked.

Leon explained that Shirley's voice was special. He wanted to train her in a certain way—and singing with a group might spoil it. He did not want to take any chances with that voice!

One Sunday morning when she was five, she sang her first solo in church. It was scary—but fun. And the smile on her father's face told her he was enormously proud of her.

"It's going to be solos from now on," he said to Shirley's mother on the way home from church. "She's not going to get up there in that choir with a lot of people and ruin that voice!"

In 1938 Leon Verrett made up his mind to leave New Orleans. His children were going to segregated schools because they were Negro, and he was worried about their education and the jobs they would be able to get when they graduated. California was booming. He was sure that, as a building contractor, he would have more opportunities there than in the Deep South. Moving West could mean a good life for all the family.

The Verretts settled in Oxnard, outside Los Angeles, and Shirley entered Seventh-Day Adventist school. During her years in grammar and high school she sang regularly in church and informally for friends. Once when the famous Negro choir director Hall Johnson was in Los Angeles, Shirley had a chance to sing for him. He was greatly impressed both by the quality of her mezzo-soprano voice and her ability to express the feeling of the songs.

"Someday you'll have a great success," he told her. "But whatever you do in life, in your singing or in anything else, remember this, hurry slowly."

Hurry slowly. . . . What he was really saying was, *Take pains with what you do. Don't rush ahead without planning.* A career, especially in the arts, had to be shaped step by step.

It happened, though, that whenever the subject of a singing career was mentioned at home, her father bristled. Singing on the stage was not for a daughter of his. He felt that a voice like hers should express things of the spirit. If Shirley wanted to train for something it should be business. And why not real estate? As a contractor, he knew the opportunities for bright young men and women in the field. With Shirley's outgoing personality—and that smile—she was bound to be a success!

Ventura Junior College gave a two-year course in liberal arts and business administration, and Shirley enrolled there after graduating from high school. One evening when her Spanish teacher was giving a party, students were asked to entertain, to do "whatever you do best."

Shirley sang a spiritual and the teacher was amazed by the power and quality of her voice. Word of this talent spread through school, and she became the singing star of Ventura's concerts.

After completing the two-year course, she received her Associate in Arts degree in 1951 and took the California real-estate examination to get her license. With Mr. Verrett's help she went into a real-estate office and settled down to showing homes and writing contracts.

People coming in to ask about property were impressed by this tall (5′ 6″), handsome girl with the beautiful speaking voice. She was brisk and efficient and there was a sincerity in her selling that made people remember her. Customers who bought a house from Shirley Verrett often sent their friends to her too.

The future looked bright. California was outstripping New York in population, and selling real estate there was bound to be profitable. Shirley's friends considered her lucky. She was a gifted singer—a natural who could thrill an audience. She had a quick business mind. And she had recently been married. Everything looked fine—on the outside.

But things were not going well. The marriage was not a happy one. She and her husband had agreed to a divorce. Furthermore, she was not satisfied working in real estate. Shirley wanted to sing—not just at recitals and concerts in the Los Angeles area but professionally.

But what to do about it? Fly to New York and announce her arrival to concert managers in the hope that they would sign her immediately for recitals, records, the Metropolitan Opera?

Unfortunately, New York was swamped with talented

singers—young men and women who had taken years of the most expensive voice training. Even *they* had a hard time winning recognition. Competing against them meant she would have to devote full time to singing. It could not be her second interest anymore; it had to be first.

By putting it at the center of her life and pouring all her energies into it, she might make Hall Johnson's prediction come true.

Friends recommended a voice teacher—Anna Fitziu—in Hollywood and Shirley Verrett studied with her for five months. Her progress was so rapid that an appearance on the Arthur Godfrey television show, "Talent Scouts," was arranged. The Godfrey show, which was carried by one of the networks and seen by millions across the country, was considered a first-rate showcase for talented beginners who were on the brink of making a name professionally.

"If Godfrey gives you a spot on his show and you do well, good things can happen," Shirley's friends told her.

She flew to New York—with her parents' good wishes—and began rehearsing her song, "My Heart at Thy Sweet Voice," an aria from the opera *Samson and Delilah*. A week later she sang it before the television cameras. And good things did happen! A call came from Mme. Marian Freschl of the famous Juilliard School of Music inviting Shirley to study voice with her and to try for a scholarship at the institute.

"I think I can arrange it," Mme. Freschl said. "You have a rare voice—but for concert work and opera it must be trained. For this you must work hard!"

Shirley Verrett was accepted at Juilliard as a scholarship student in autumn, 1955, and plunged into a routine that was exhilarating—and exhausting. Ventura Junior College had given her liberal-arts courses and business training. At Juilliard she concentrated on music exclusively. The institute, later to move to the Lincoln Center complex, was then located on upper Broadway, just north of Columbia University. In warm weather when the windows were open the whole area rang with music being produced by the students. Piano and percussion, strings and brass could be heard—in varying keys and varying tempos. But all *fortissimo!*

To be accepted for study at Juilliard was a signal honor. The teachers—most of them noted musicians and conductors —never had trouble getting students to do their homework.

All enrollees took certain basic courses—music history, for instance—and then concentrated on their specialty: composing, conducting, an instrument, or voice. Voice students took lessons from a man or woman who could give them not only superior technical training but the benefit of years as a professional.

Madame Freschl was such a teacher. With her years of experience she worked out a long-range plan for Shirley that would take her, step by step, to success on the concert stage and—perhaps—opera as well.

Analyzing Shirley's voice, she found that it was a classical mezzo (low) soprano but with a wide "spectrum" from steady low, through velvety middle, up to a strong, clear high B.

The voice is an instrument, she pointed out, that is as sensitive as a violin. Like a violin, it could give out squawks—if used clumsily! On the other hand, it could pour out glorious melody when the right techniques and controls were applied.

"Try it again, Shirley," she would say. "I want to hear the notes come easily and naturally, to be in *gola*—in the throat."

Standing beside the concert grand piano in the studio, Shirley would sing the aria again. Sometimes it was just a phrase she worked on, over and over.

Madame Freschl was a perfectionist. "I know you can

produce beautiful *tones,* Shirley, but we want them to make musical sense. Can you project what the tones mean? Can you get inside the music?"

Training the voice was a painstaking business. Marian Anderson, the great Negro contralto, had studied years before winning success. Gladys Swarthout, who like Shirley was a mezzo-soprano, took lessons from the time she was ten years old until she was twenty-three before winning bit parts in the Chicago Opera.

Shirley was starting late. Many voice coaches would have discouraged her. She not only had to become master of her voice as an "instrument" but had to learn opera roles and concert songs in Italian, French, and German.

When she was tempted to be anxious about the years of formal training she had missed, Shirley remembered Hall Johnson's advice: *Hurry slowly.* Madame Freschl lived by the same principle. She reminded her pupil that breath control and voice projection could not be learned in a "cram" course!

For the first two years at Juilliard, Shirley Verrett's singing was limited to amateur performances: student recitals and parts in the opera workshop. Her first chance to sing professionally came in the summer of 1957. She sang roles in two modern operas, *Lost in the Stars* (based on the novel *Cry, The Beloved Country!*) and *The Rape of Lucretia* at Antioch College in Ohio.

The next season when *Lost in the Stars* was being prepared by the New York City Opera Company she won the role of Irinia and made her first paid appearance in New York.

A big goal came next: a New York recital. When a singer feels that he is ready to leave the amateur ranks and become a full-fledged professional, he books a recital hall, sells tickets, and invites the newspaper critics to judge and review the performance.

A recital debut announces to the world, "I am now good

enough to be paid for my concerts. My apprenticeship is over."

If a singer scores with the critics on the night of his recital debut he is well launched on a career. On November 4, 1958, Shirley made her debut at Town Hall. The next morning the critic for *The New York Times* called her an "earnest, conscientious singer" who showed the "results of careful preparation."

Another newspaper critic was more generous: "She is a mezzo with none of the vocal mannerisms so typical of the species: of gonging and throbbing from the chest she does none. Nor does she hoot as she moves upwards to the top of her range."

The voice of this newcomer, he concluded, ". . . is dark-hued, but she can snap it bright and sunny on command."

She was not a spectacular talent yet. But the New York musical world knew there was a Shirley Verrett.

The 1958 Town Hall recital came at the midpoint in her studies at Juilliard. She had enrolled three years before and was to take another three years to complete requirements for her "Diploma in Voice."

With the faculty's approval she was allowed to stretch out her program of studies beyond the usual term so that she could make concert appearances out of town. Singing professionally was necessary for two reasons: She could polish before an audience what she had learned in school; and concerts meant money for living expenses.

Her capacity for winning scholarships and awards was almost a legend at Juilliard. Her prizes totaled more than $25,000 in the six years at the music institute.

After her debut, offers to sing with symphonic orchestras began to come—in a trickle at first but eventually increasing to a flood. She worked easily with conductors and became a favorite soloist with top orchestras. When the venerable Leopold Stokowski was invited to return to lead the Philadelphia Orchestra after being absent nineteen years he picked the tall, poised soprano to appear with him. Dynamic Leonard Bernstein chose her to sing with the New York Philharmonic when the orchestra gave its first concert at Philharmonic Hall in the newly opened Lincoln Center.

An offer from the Metropolitan Opera came soon afterward, but Shirley turned it down.

"I'll sing at the Met someday," she wrote her parents, "but I want to pick my own role—probably Carmen."

A chance to sing Carmen at Spoleto, Italy, came in the summer of 1962. But the critics were lukewarm.

"She gave glimpses of the excellent Carmen she will be one day," said one. "She has the warm vibrant voice and earthy womanliness for it."

In 1963 she again sang the role, this time in Moscow at the Bolshoi Opera House. While Don José and all other characters sang in Russian, Shirley sang the title role in French! The Russian audience, nevertheless, was so impressed that they gave her a twenty-minute standing ovation. This vibrant young American made Bizet's gypsy come alive for them. If she had been singing in Swahili it would still have thrilled them.

Returning to New York, she appeared on the Ed Sullivan television program, singing the "Habanera" from *Carmen*. At home in Los Angeles her family clustered around the set to watch her, now near the peak of her career, as they had once watched prayerfully eight years before when she tried out on "Talent Scouts."

The year 1963 was important for a personal reason also. On December 10 she was married to Louis Lo Monaco, an artist teaching at the Parsons School of Design. To accommodate both careers, they took a handsome, oversize apartment in Manhattan overlooking the Hudson River. Here Shirley was able to vocalize in the living room while her husband painted or operated his printmaking machine in his studio-den down the hall.

Her career was so well established by this time that she

was making almost 100 concert and opera appearances each year. RCA Victor signed her to record both full-length operas and opera highlights. She did aι. album of religious music, "How Great Thou Art, Precious Lord," and one called "Singin' in the Storm," featuring folk and protest songs.

"Will you sing at the Met someday, Shirley?" her father asked in a letter.

"When the right time comes," she answered. "When I have a chance to do *my* role."

It came in 1968. Shirley signed a contract to sing Carmen in the first week of the Metropolitan Opera's schedule.

Opera is the most complex, most demanding form of expression for singers. In a recital they are alone on a stage with a pianist, and voice carries them. Even when they do solo work with a great symphony orchestra, voice carries them. But opera combines singing with acting and puts tremendous demands on its stars.

Shirley Verrett had sung the role of Carmen half a dozen times in Europe, in Canada, and with the New York City Opera Company. She understood the personality of the fiery gypsy woman completely and had long ago mastered the dramatic fireworks that make the role come alive. But when she reported for rehearsals at the Metropolitan Opera House and looked at the scenery for her production she was stunned. A semicircular bullring, needed for the climax, was to be onstage throughout. All the singing and acting would have to be done in and around it . . . as if it were invisible to the actors and audience!

Even worse, she would have to sing the famous "Habanera" halfway up a set of steep steps at the rear of the stage where the orchestra would be hard to hear. And she would have to do her gypsy dance atop a tiny round table!

Rehearsals on such a cluttered stage were beginning to strain the nerves of both Shirley and her costar, Jon Vickers, playing Don José. At the final dress rehearsal when Vickers was acting out a stage "fight" with Carmen and knocked her to the floor, Shirley suddenly had an inspiration. When Don José's back was turned, she got up and moved, getting ready for her next aria. Vickers turned to sing to her and found himself staring at the floor. He was furious. "If you start improvising now, I'll improvise on opening night!" he thundered.

Angry and embarrassed, Shirley had an immediate impulse to shout back. But she decided to keep cool and take it in stride. As she later told her husband, "I said to myself, 'Shirley, be a lady. Keep quiet. After all, it's his scene.'"

On the night of the performance, the fight scene went off without a hitch. Carmen stayed in place, exactly in the spot where Don José had thrown her.

When the last curtain fell and the stars appeared for curtain calls, the audience gave Shirley Verrett rousing applause. As she came out time and again for curtain calls, she flashed smiles to people in the balconies, the Grand Tier, the boxes. Then her eyes rested for an instant on a certain row in the orchestra. There, three seats in from the center aisle, a handsome man in a tuxedo and a beaming woman in evening gown and fur stole were clapping harder than anyone else in the audience: Leon and Elvira Verrett.

Their daughter's voice *was* special. Leon Verrett had known it years ago in New Orleans. But as for singing at the Metropolitan Opera House—he had not dared to go *that* high. It was Shirley herself who had taken the risk and done the hard work.

At a party later that night at the St. Regis Hotel, Shirley Verrett was asked if she had suffered any special jitters before going onstage.

She admitted that she had, but quickly got them under control. "When you've worked up to the right peak, you just get out on that stage and sing!"

MARTHE GROSS was born in St. Louis, Missouri, and attended school there. While in high school she tried ice-skating and tennis—unsuccessfully—and writing for the school paper—successfully. In her senior year she convinced her mother that they could make a brilliant success of opening a flower shop, an enterprise that proved financially disastrous. A business failure at twenty-one, she decided to enroll at Washington University as a journalism major. Feature stories which she wrote for the college paper were reprinted by the *St. Louis Globe-Democrat,* which later hired her as a cub reporter.

Having proved that she could write professionally, she came to New York and has lived and worked there ever since. Her jobs have included magazine reporting (one assignment took her cruising the Eastern seaboard in an ad-flashing blimp), radio news writing for the Voice of America, and editing for "Today's Secretary," published by the Gregg Division of McGraw-Hill. More recently she has divided her time between teaching English at Long Island high schools and writing articles for a number of magazines including *Parents', Good Housekeeping, The Christian Herald, Together, Cue,* and *Quest.*

She is the wife of Murray Gross—who also began his business career as a cub reporter—and is the mother of two sons, William and Matthew.